The Sixth Out Of Seven Series

Book One

Triumphant Through My Early Years

Jannette Barrett

MARCIA M
PUBLISHING HOUSE

Triumphant Through My Early Years
The Sixth Out Of Seven Series
Authored by Jannette Barrett
©copyright Jannette Barrett 2018

Cover Design Marcia M Publishing House
Photographs are the property of the author Jannette Barrett

Edited by Marcia M Spence, advised by Jonathan Partington with Marcia M
Publishing House Editorial Team Published by Marcia M Spence of Marcia M
Publishing House, Oldbury, West Midlands the UNITED KINGDOM B69

*The content in this book will be emotionally and intellectually challenging to engage with.
There are especially graphic or intense content that represents child abuse experienced by
the author.*

MARCIA M
PUBLISHING HOUSE

www.marciampublishing.com

Book One
Triumphant Through My Early Years

Is as the title states, an overcoming.
To write it, I had to regress to those years of realising
I was neglected and face again the fact I was abused.
Many don't acknowledge the fact
they were abused until much older,
in some ways I've been envious of others
as I've lived my whole life knowing
that I was indeed abused, and it affected me
at every stage of my life.

Jannette Barrett

Why Would It Matter If I Got Hurt Anyway?

*Lots of toys kisses and cuddles, by 6pm
a bath full of bubbles.
Nice if that's how it had been, not so for me,
I saw what I should never have seen.*

*There was love shown yes in the strangest of ways,
Love through discipline throughout those early days.
"Don't do that! You might get hurt."
Then a whack across my back that threw me
in the dirt, that did hurt.
It hurt more than if I was left and allowed to fall,
I would have at least had some fun before.*

*A strange way to look at things I know but the discipline
shown to me was not the right way to go.
That treehouse was my open door to a life other than my
own that's for sure, to not be allowed to play in it each day,
I wasn't listening to that no way!*

*Why would it matter if I got hurt anyway?
Oh yes, who would do all those shitty jobs each day.
Seems they only saw me when there was something to do,
Seems they only saw me if none of the others were bothered
to come through.*

*School is where I wanted to be but soon even that
wasn't sanctuary.
Where's my space then? Where can it be!
Where can I relax and just be me?......*

Jannette Barrett aka Ms Lyricist B

Jannette Barrett

Dedication

I dedicate my first book to you the reader and any souls out there who resonate with my story and want to be set free to find a way to move forward against many odds.

Writing has been my Morphine Drive, my drug of survival…

The therapy that writing gave me, can be yours too.

In my Afterword I valiantly share why and how I did it by highlighting those therapeutic benefits in hope I might inspire you the reader and many others to try it.

It wasn't an easy ride, but it's been an epic release that has indelibly helped me write the following first Part of my Memoirs, 'Triumphant Through My Early Years' Book one and the Books two and three.

Jannette Barrett

<u>Special Acknowledgement</u>

St Mary's C of E School, Handsworth
West Midlands, England.
Mrs. Hackett, Mrs. Rudder, and Mr. Stanly
Sheila Maria's School of Dance
The Begum and Gayle families
And not forgetting the formidable Ms. Campbell
and her knowledgeable daughter, Yvette.

Author's Personal Acknowledgements

My Almighty Creator, I was doubtful and lacked self-confidence like Moses, but as with him, you gifted me to speak as Aaron. Personally, you lead me from my inverted captivity, through my wilderness of discontentment, and delivered me to lead by example, with my influences, rather than as an authoritarian.

Now, I care and create in my field with confidence. Unbeknown due to ignorance, I was such an angry, arrogant child, but you stayed with me through all my turmoils, making each encounter a development of my character, rather than a destroyer. I humbly accept, to You be the glory, and thank You for all those I have influenced to come to You.

To my Siblings whom I urge to read, I don't believe we are where we should be because we were all moulded by the circumstance that has blocked our pathways.

My Husband, who is my rock, my king; and my children, I sincerely thank you.

My Children, if you get an inclination on why I said, did, or indeed did not do certain things and incur an essence of understanding as to why I reacted indifferently; all the pain on unraveling this incite to myself would have been worth it. I hope from the read you all at least realise Mommy really did try her best.

The thing about facing my truths however, I had to be prepared to face it all, no matter how ugly it got.

Jannette Barrett

About the Author

WHO AM I? I am Jannette Barrett Aka Ms. Lyricist 'B' Daughter of Mr. Anthony and Mrs. Joyce Joseph.

I am the sixth child out of seven in our family. Below I am the second top left with the black collared shirt.

Photograph taken in 1999, to mark the eve of the new millennium

I was born, raised and still reside in Handsworth Birmingham UK. An original *front line*, grounded *salt of the earth ghetto gal* and I ain't in no way shape or form going to apologise for my roots.

I'm the kind of woman that would get up at a party and dance to anything, some will join in while others will stare and remark critically, but I wouldn't give two hoots at what they thought now. When I was younger however approval was what I sought and I tried desperately to attain it often in vain.

Today I'm fairly successful, I have a very worthwhile profession as a freelance mental health community worker, my business has helped many lost individuals and provided well needed respite for families. I wear my heart on my sleeve which has led me to get involved in several charity events, doing fun runs up to half marathons.

This photograph was taken at an Awards Ceremony.
I was a Finalist for MBCCA Carer of The Year Award in 2016.

Foreword
By Mr. David Solomon

"I vividly remember the first day I met Jannette. My Mom had just come home from some months in hospital. She had had a fall and was very frightened to be returning home alone, less able than she had been and needed both personal care and kindness. Jannette was highly recommended to us and came for an interview. I answered the bell to a smart and lovely lady, we knew straight away that she was the person we wanted.

Jannette put in place a professional and caring team as she couldn't accommodate all the care hours Mom needed by herself. This same team; along with Jannette, have been caring for my Mom ever since. Mom could not have done better; she always received the best of care and I knew that she was in safe hands with just the right mix of kindness and understanding. This so much reflects upon Jan herself, as the kind of person you would want always at your side.

Jannette became a trusted friend. Though our backgrounds could hardly have been more different; we found we had a lot in common, so when she honoured me by showing me the early first draft of her autobiography, I knew this was a story that must be told; it's raw and often painful. Jannette has been through so much that would flatten a lesser person.

I know there were times when she doubted that she should carry on with it.

There will be parts in there that you will find uncomfortable reading, but as she is such a kind person, she tries to take you through it with essences of counsel.

In the end then, you see that in her determination she shines through, there is always hope. I strongly commend this book to you as I commend my friend Jannette."

Book One

Triumphant Through My Early Years

Jannette Barrett

Jannette Barrett

CHAPTER ONE

JUST WANTING MY FAIR SHARE

Seven children coming practically year after year, *Oh dear, poor Mother.* I imagine her pregnant with Pam, (she is the last), me in her arms, Sarah tugging at her skirt tail for something or other, Jenna trying to put her clothes on but getting it wrong, just us four would mean simultaneous, morning sickness, terry nappies, potty training, and bed wetting. Never mind Sheila, Martha and Desmond who were older.

Desmond is our only brother and the firstborn, then came all us sisters. Gosh, he must've been so fed up seeing mom come home with baby girl, after girl, after girl, and never a baby boy to be his brother.

As children, there was certainly a pecking order to adhere to, first Desmond, then Martha, Sheila, Jenna, Sarah, myself Jannette and then Pam. As I was almost last, it wasn't much fun for me that's for sure.

Remember team picking at school! Did you ever feel sorry for the last one chosen? Hello, that was usually me in this case, the last one standing and not for heroic reasons.

We had lots of confusion and chaos seemed to materialise from nothing, molehills became mountains. I suppose we were just too close in age with every one of us obstinate and headstrong.

Dad ruled us with a rod of iron! A broom handle, a thick leather belt soaked in his own piss and a short piece of curtain wire or whatever he could lay his hands on to inflict pain. Not rod was spared, we were certainly not spoilt children. Living in an environment where everyone had to fight for their survival, where there was a pecking order that started years before me, I was lucky to even be noticed.

So, I developed the art of exaggeration. And dramatisation. I became fully aware that I had to do that to be seen, I would accentuate my cleaning up almost acting it out as if on stage with huge elaborate arm movements and sighs anything for attention. Have you ever noticed when a child catches your eye whilst they are doing something, they really want approval for?

See how they turn up the volume on their voice and over exaggerate whatever it is they're doing! This was my survival tool.

As a child, I was often placed in situations that scared me, yet they too have empowered and built me. It's these scenarios they say that determine the strength of character you portray later in adult life.

Who's thinking about strength, character building, or any of that empowering stuff as a child though?! All I wanted was my fair share, equivalent to what the others got at least.

What I obtained sadly was not fair, threadbare clothes was part of my lot. Clothes handed down from sister number one to two to three to four and then to me sister number five. When I had finished with them they were often too far gone for Pam, my younger sister so on occasion she got new clothes. I felt cross when she got some new ones as I never did.

I'll have you know, the material was so shiny from the constant pressing with those old-fashioned irons, no steam, just father's spit, (yes, father did do the ironing, I'll get to that a little later) that they used to attract so much static, mainly because most of them were made from polyester or nylon, oh it played havoc against my woollen tights I can tell you, plus they were always too big. I hated having the sleeves rolled up and the waist held in with a huge nappy pin.

Nothing was wasted, *'mend and make do'* was Mom and Dad's motto, quite right too.

I never knew how hard it was for them to make ends meet did I? So yes, I dragged my heels and sulked.

Pre-worn hand me down shoes were the worst thing, the heels, Oh My God! They should have had a hazard warning attached. They were so lean that you could easily have broken your ankles trying to keep balance whilst walking.

The amount of times I buckled them, I'm amazed I didn't break one. Aesthetically pleasing! Oh yes, if you wanted to look like you had bow legs. As if that wasn't enough, inserted were the neatly cut out cardboard linings made by Mother's skilful hands, they made my feet sweaty, yuck!

In my very first year at primary school we were told to prepare for P.E, physical education.

"Come on now boys and girls, change down to your vest and pants put on your plimsoles then line up at the door so I can take you down to the hall."

Said our teacher, I had no problem doing that as everyone was doing the same, so I simply followed suit. We were all taught to put our clothes in our desk, I took pride in folding mine neatly looking at the teacher for her approval which I got.

"Everyone look at Jannette see how neat and tidy she's placing her clothes in the desk," but then I got to the point when I had to remove my tights.

I pulled my feet out of my shoes and attached to my woolen tights was the cardboard only now due to my sweaty feet it was soft and shredding just in view of another pupil.

"Ahh hah hah, what's that?" Said the girl right next to me, I found myself jumping up and down to play the clown using my art of exaggeration, showing them off even more and picking at them then flicking bits so that she could laugh, I wasn't laughing I was dying inside, embarrassment don't cut it, I can tell you.

One-minute approval then the next... I can only describe it as the look when you forget to take the tissues out of your pocket and it's all over the washing, that was how my tights were, just as if they were tarred and feathered.

Anyway, back to the shoes, thank goodness for 'Blakeys' when Mom went to the cobblers and got introduced to those steel crescent shaped caps that stopped the heel wearing down; I had to attach them to my heels and bang them against the concrete doorstep, it was our saving grace. Yes, sir, whoever invented them, I'm sure they made a killing.

Mom always bought 'Clark's shoes' to begin with, so they were going to last until your toes were 'begging for bread,' I'm sure you can visualise, the print of toes, changing the true form of the shoe, I certainly have an idea of how those Japanese Geisha women felt with their feet bound. I wonder what Mother thought when he showed them to her?

Knowing Mother, she would have said, in patois something along the lines of,

"laard a mercie, why dem neva cum out wid dis ya sumting donkey ears ago, mi cudda save mi self a whole heap a money, boat mi a trow weh mi good shoes dem wen life still pon top, afta' all is only de heel was a give weh."

My Mother was so conservative in her undertaking never would she waste money. Since they were cheaper than buying new shoes, she would be getting them, that's for sure. A great pity there was no substitute for the worn insoles and pending holes, cardboard Mother really?!

Blakeys were absolutely phenomenal, it made those worn out shoes just about bearable with its click! Everyone unlucky enough to have to wear them, purposely walked extra hard to emphasise their clicking noise.

Ha! I'm laughing now at the attempts of tap dancing; it became such a popular pastime to hide one's embarrassment. I, of course, exaggerated as usual and had to sing as well as dance. I sang only to prevent my nervous laughter, in case they saw the print of my toes in the shoes get my drift!

Fair share that's all I ever wanted.

Now try to imagine how I felt seeing new items of clothes come into our house all crisp and clean looking.

They were certainly always good quality stuff, had to be; Mother wasn't going to buy something that wouldn't last.

I remember how I almost salivated over some of Martha and Sheila's clothes. I really wanted to have them, then that day would arrive, only by then they were all ragged and roughed up by the time they got to me.

"Here you are, these are yours now, they still have a bit of use left."

"Thank you, Mommy."

I would begrudgingly hold out my hands to Mother's arms lined with beautiful floral orange and pink chiffon sleeves belonging to an elegant blouse, take the pile of clothes containing, washed out corduroy trousers with rubbed out knees, greyish old shirts with frayed collars, supposed to be white of course, and a velvet skirt with no pile left to it, basically a pile of old tatt. I'd hold them to my chest and think, "this ain't no fair share, not fair at all."

We had cousins; I don't know if they were richer than us or simply the fact there were less of them. Every now and then they came to our house with a black bin liner of their unwanted clothing; oh, you should have seen our eyes, we looked like 'John crow.' It's a word Jamaicans use for vultures.

We sat poised, just as a vulture would waiting for leftovers looking at the bag fat and bulging, thinking when would it be passed to us? Mother never gave them to us in front of our cousins of course. Oh no, far too much pride for that, we would simply have died of embarrassment.

In the kitchen they would sit around the table, Mother would have laid out her best lace tablecloth prior to their arrival and be wearing her bright yellow apron with the frilly edging.

On the table would be one of Dad's cakes, as soon as they arrived, they would be escorted through to the kitchen just in case one of us embarrassed Mother by saying the wrong thing.

Inside, out of site they would have the usual catch up chat over a cup of tea in the best china of course, we could hear Mother laughing posh, it wasn't her real laugh. They would chat for about an hour before they would be off again only having a brief chat with us.

After that wait which made us even more eager and the bag was passed to us, we dived in like our lives depended on it, we rummaged and pulled, it was a tug of war when an item was held by two of us. I don't know how none of the garments ripped.

It was tough on us younger ones, so I don't know why I'm smiling whilst recalling this, but I find I am. Maybe it's because I can also see the parade, catwalk style as we tried things on wiggling our bottoms and pushing out our chests, we were all however particularly keen on the shoes.

"Jenna where do you think you're going? Nothing ain't gonna fit you, unless it's something off auntie Hilary!" Laughed Sheila, I'm telling you Sheila had no filter.

"So, who said I'm looking for clothes! I want shoes so there."

Our cousins really loved their shoes, not a sensible pair in sight, if only you saw my sisters trying to squeeze their feet into the pretty pairs. I certainly had my Cinderella moment, watching that.

"Give me that one Sheila I've already got the other foot."

"No way you give that one to me you can't get your big foot in those."

Poor Martha, nice hair sis, but man, your feet let you down; big and completely flat, they were only a size 7 mind you, but Sheila knew hers were a bit smaller and made sure she took advantage of that fact.

So funny Martha is, the names she calls herself, *'the duckbilled platypus'* amongst other things, that animal really has the flattest feet ever. We really know how to take the mickey out of ourselves with our own name calling, our lethal defence, if someone else did it though…

Good memories, great to remember things like that, when I also recall all the other stuff that was rather shitty to be honest.

We really were highly creative with those clothes, changing them to get them to fit, at least we tried to be. It does scare me sometimes my memory, how real and in my face it gets.

I was sitting in a pram with my sister Pam once, we were outside but that's not unusual it was a common practice of the time to leave youngsters in their prams to get some fresh air and settle but I was placed there to pacify her.

The thing is, I was only about twenty-six or so months of age, just over two and she's eleven months younger, but also autistic, I was left in charge of her I'll never understand why or forget the experience.

This memory is so profound and deeply overwhelming for me, that the only way I can tell it clearly is to write it poetically.

Sitting in a Pram with Pam

I was sitting in a pram with my sister Pam
only placed there to pacify her.
I tapped my bare feet upon her chest to hush her
as she was restless.
I remember it so vividly as I have such ticklish feet,
my laugh I had to fight as my toes she tried to bite.

Mother came out with a bottle propped her up and said,
'make sure she doesn't choke, or the pillow drops from
behind her head,' then Mother went back inside.
I looked over the side of the pram, my drink must also be
coming; so, I held my hands out high,
'where's my drink Mommy? Here am I.'
My hands grew tired, so I rested them in my lap, whilst my
feet continued of course to tap! tap! tap.

I heard my sister supping on that bottle teat, oh the milk she
was drinking looked ever so sweet.
'Where's my drink Mommy, where's my drink?'
It's been a long time now, so my brain began to think.
'Is there no drink for me! I'm thirsty Mommy please look
I'm doing my duty.'

Slurp! Slurps! My sister is sucking on air obviously she's
finished her drink now, this is so unbelievably unfair.
'Where's my drink Mommy, wwwhere's my dddrink?'

Some other memories are just as profound triggers; shapes, smells, colours, especially those flipping dirty beige coloured trousers that my uncle wore, along with his bulging zip, that memory is a parasite.

Memories of that nature so deeply negative I put them in the same category as '*Japanese Knotweed*' those roots entangle and strangle anything in its path. My negatives did the same to me, they spread through me like a virus. Like spores they multiplied and occupied all my positive energies clothing me in a darkness that diminished my true light.

The effects of it took over my whole life I had multiple negative memories. They made me feel as though I was constantly shallow breathing and that my true essence was depleted.

Mother got muddled with our names, not sure why because they are all vastly different, not even the sounds of them are similar. She would almost go through the lot before reaching mine sometimes it was simply "one of you."

So, down the line it went from Desmond to Martha to Sheila Jenna then Sarah.

"I'm not going" said Desmond, this was repeated by my older siblings until I felt myself being pushed forward, "guess it's me again then." "I'm coming Mommy."

See, the pecking order was not much fun for me at all was it?

It wouldn't even have been that bad if it wasn't for the sniggering when the rest got away with it. It was always one of those nasty chores like separating the washing, the bin cleaning, or doing Dad's feet.

Got three children of our own now, my husband and I, a daughter and two sons. I had them four to five years apart, I say I, because I had my first two who were not entirely planned before my current husband of over twenty odd years, although we have been together longer.

I am pleased it panned out that way because I wouldn't have wanted to struggle like Mother by having them too close and I certainly wouldn't have wanted them to fight.

Oh, come on now don't get me wrong, I loved and respected her for being able to get through. At one point she and Dad would have coped with all of us from a new born baby to a pre-teen at the start of senior school age one to eleven; I just know I couldn't do that.

Back then, lots of couples had six or more children. One set of our cousins in fact is a family of nine children; I should say seven now as two have sadly passed on.

It wasn't just that though, if the others took some of the brunt of caring for Pam, I mean she could be so loving and endearing, I wouldn't have minded or been so resentful and angry.

There was a time, when Pam and I got stuck under the bed because we were playing in my brother's room where we certainly shouldn't have been, and he walked in.

"Pam shush," I whispered.

Pam found it so funny skinning her teeth so much her whole body was shaking, "I'm coming on top of you then."

I lay on top of Pam for what seemed an hour, whilst she wriggled under me like a worm, she just didn't understand the consequences of being caught, thank goodness he was only looking for some yard (home) clothes to put on.

When Desmond eventually left his room, Pam and I laughed and laughed then hugged each other with relief, now that was a special moment indeed.

My whole life revolved around Pam, I was her main carer, my needs did not get noticed, this made me feel invisible. The fact that she has learning disabilities held me in a vicious circle of dislike of myself and the situations I was placed in. I love my sister dearly, and I love Ice Cream, but I wouldn't want to eat it every day for my three meals.

Can you understand why I was left responsible for my sister at such a young age when I had four more sisters who were older? Would you have been resentful too?

I'm jumping back and forth somewhat, please stay with me. It's just that there's a great deal of sensitive stuff in my head and I'm trying to give myself counsel whilst I write, and I guess I'm also looking for some justification too, to understand my feelings and actions,

Memory, it's a past experience, isn't it? So, I must be realistic in thinking that perhaps sometimes I may have become clouded over it, I know a considerable part of it was horrid and I suppose as my life has really been challenging certainly a labored catalogue of lessons; all I now know has made me the resilient person I am.

Dad ruled us in many ways and our age didn't come into the equation not one iota. I couldn't have been more than three when he decided that my punishment for allowing Pam to smear the skirting boards with the Cherry Blossom shoe polish was to use my fluffy barnet (yes my hair!) as a scrubbing brush to remove it, when it was all clean, my head was full of *'coco bumps'* that's a term we Jamaicans use when we get a raised lump come up like a volcano from a bad knock to the head.

Daddy knocked my head and rubbed it against that skirting board so many times, I could even see with my wide stretched eyes and through the tears that he was finding it difficult to stay down that low, yet he continued to violently punish me.

It made me so dizzy.

Then after cleaning the boards, he proceeded to bend me over the bath and scrub my hair forcefully with carbolic soap which went into my eyes stinging them to temporary blindness, my head and eyes were so very sore when he finished.

At the end of this, once he finally allowed me to go, I deliberately banged the front of my head against the bedroom door, in an attempt to knock myself out so I could sleep off the pain.

I remember it all.

Counsellors and therapists often ask, "how was your childhood?"

Well mine was *Shit, Shit, Shitty* a lot of the time, that childhood blueprint really is my scaffolding. I guess my scaffolding missed some interlocking links because I fell off the planks a good few times and symbolically scraped my knees.

Our family was strong mind you, we certainly learnt everything the hard way, so amongst our dysfunction, it made us tight. Tight against others I mean, if anyone dared to interfere in our lives or cause harm, we would show our true grit and defend each other.

I can put hand on heart and say, if any of my siblings are in need, I will offer my hand, my ear, and my sincerity. We all would in our individual kind of way. I am proud of this, it is my sibling badge of loyalty.

Six girls so close in age and all headstrong meant trouble, *poor Mother*. I know I keep saying this, but I just couldn't do what she did, all those heads of hair to comb, no wonder she looked for help. Two in the bathtub sometimes three, same scenario in bed. My little sister and I would watch the chaos of the daily routine knowing we were free from the rush of the morning because we were too young for school.

I loved to watch Mother rake through my sisters' heads of hair from roots to tips, locking each of her daughters in with her strong thighs and powerful wide hips.

"Sit still Sheila your head tuff, give mi de grease so mi can smood de ruff."

"Mommy I can do it myself now you know,"

"Weh yu a seh! Like yestadeh wen yu wark out like poppy show."

Mother slaps on a handful of green pomade, greases the front so that it even shines in the shade. Rake, rake, then rake some more two with two plaits another with more.

"One, two, three of yu done," Mother keeps score, "last one cum, I have wuk to get to."

I just watched and sniggered it was payback time, they left me scraps and passed the buck. "Hah hah," it's me now laughing they ran out of luck.

Oh, such a little rascal was I and at not quite four, an old head on young shoulders and cunning as a fox.

This daily occurrence never changed much until Martha and Sheila sort of branched off. Being slightly older, they became capable of conducting their own affairs in the art of school preparation. With this, I looked for something else I could get excited about, the visual morning display of chaos was now boring.

Each day after all that morning prep came hush! The front door closed here began the best part of my day. My exciting time had arrived, it was all about me now, finally in charge.

Every room became my playground at least for a couple of hours before the dreaded Mrs. Campbell arrived. She came because obviously we couldn't be left all day.

As I was nearly four, I thought I didn't need her that much anymore. We had her looking after us since time began. Mother had to work so it was good that she found someone to sit with us, I suppose.

Two hours of caring for Pam in the mornings was more than enough for me to cope with, she could look after Pam. Yes, I didn't mind that, but stubborn me didn't like my playground being disrupted. The house was mine until she came and burst my bubble, thinking I was big at four, honestly.

The Tree House and Me

My house was colossal in size, and there were three double sash windows to the top. Two even bigger ones with their own framed coving left and right of an enormous white wooden door that had two thin stained coloured glass windows of its own. The number displayed was 44 and the street, St Peters Road.

The brass knocker holder and letterbox were always kept highly polished along with the pillar-box red doorstep. Mother took great pride in the appearance of our house it was her pride and joy.

Each side of the door protruded a concrete pillar with an engraved overhanging roof, some kind of porch of the day, I expect, certainly handy to protect you from the rain. Leading to the front door there were three steps from the path. Wow! It really was a very big house indeed.

It wasn't their first house, Mom and Dad lived together somewhere else before, but then they began to have us, a bigger house soon became a necessity, no complaints there.

The houses in those days with their Victorian, Georgian or Edwardian features were built much bigger than these modern-day new builds. Most of these properties that are still standing today have been utilised to accommodate more than one family, typically comprising of three sometimes four flats.

Our house however no longer exists, the picture above is all we have left. I wish some of my memories of it had evaporated into my deep subconscious never to emerge again. It really was a house of mixed blessings. Alas, if it had all evaporated, I guess I wouldn't have written this and come to terms with some of the most challenging periods of my life.

My keeping of the house picture is to remind me that *not all that glitters is gold.* The house held secrets and lies, along with some shameful episodes, *still waters run deep,* our murky undertones would certainly have killed all the fish.

Now, I was born in the sixties, and as you now know I'm sixth in line which means my parents along with my two eldest siblings lived there in the fifties just as more and more 'Windrush' common-wealth folk stepped on British shores for the first time.

Imagine a single black family living in predominantly white area and having an exceptionally large house. We were well established with assets and we even had our own car. Some of our kinfolk were lucky enough to get one room in a shared house, on hearing such stories we had to do our bit and help others, it's got to be the proudest part of my family history that I shall forever shout about. That's what over the years, I've found so difficult to understand, just how incredibly kind and charitable my parents could be, but yet we children endured those beatings!

My Mom and Dad decided to rent out all our top floor rooms to help our race, we were one of the only houses to not say, *No Irish, no dogs, no Blacks'* Wow! It was difficult to get somewhere to live as it was only, we and the Jews who were willing to let.

I can almost feel the delight of our people coming across our house and not seeing that sign but one saying, *'rooms for rent ALL welcome'* then Mom or Dad opening the door to them with the warmest of smiles. One family comes to mind; I think they were African because of their name, it was 'Ukunami.' I've no doubt I've spelt it incorrectly. We even had Uncle living with us too, as he was a loner, Mom and Dad took pity and gave him one of the front rooms. He hung around like a distasteful bad smell, boiled salted fish comes to my mind ingrained and penetrating.

Those years were confusing. Okay I was young and impressionable so perhaps it was a normal way of life.

Shift workers had odd hours, when one family worked another would have the room and vica- versa so much comings and goings to get by in life. They of course had to eat, so if they were working a night shift for example, they slept in the day and had their breakfast at supper time!

Anyway, like I said, there was lots happening.

Do you know, the best part of all the goings on in that huge house was that, due to me and my little sister being what the big folks thought too small to know or understand anything, we saw and heard everything. It used to be Sarah, Pam and myself left but Sarah is sixteen months older than me so when she started school, it was just Pam and me.

When the lodgers went off to work or came in and straight to their locked rooms to sleep; Mom and my siblings went off to school and work. I let my imagination run wild with the stories I heard around the house, re-enact the quarrels wagging my finger at my sister who didn't give a hoot by the way, playing the big 'I am' in Mom's jacket and shoes.

I had a lot of fun pretending to be in charge. Pam was like my very own live teddy bear,

"sit here, sit there." I'd say and she usually would. When we re-enacted the quarrels one of us would be a man and tthen we would swop.

Still wearing Mom's jacket and shoes I'd say, 'you be the mommy and I'll be the daddy okay!'

"Yyyep" she says as she grabs Mom's coat off my shoulders before I get the chance to give it to her.

"Here you are! Take the shoes as well,"

Pam always nodded her head clearly when saying yes or no as if to make sure I knew she wanted to play or didn't want to be disturbed.

"What's for dinner?" I began the pretence,

"nnnnothing, no dddinner,"

"what yah mean no dinner, I've just done twelve hours."

I don't know why but we could always hear things like that quite loudly then it all got distorted with noise, mumbled shouting and banging doors. It was great making those noises and shouting,

"arrrh bang bang crash" I would make the noises with the chair usually.

"I'm gggoing to ssstammp mmmy fffoot nnnow like mmmoommy dddoes."

Pam was the best at foot stamping.
I enjoyed the little play times we had as long as Pam wanted to play that is, because she didn't always.

When she didn't want to play, I had to somehow get her into the garden, it was safer outside than inside because when she had tantrums things could get broken and I'd be punished.

Our garden, oh, I loved that garden! It was a real treat. There was a little area for chickens; I'm not quite sure if we also had other animals, definitely chickens though.

Almost in the middle was the best most amazing thing in the whole wide world, a big Oak tree; it was simply the widest tree I'd ever seen and we lived very near to a park so we saw lots of different types of trees. The branches were chunky and came down very low so you could climb up it in seconds.

My brother with Dad's help of course, built a Treehouse in it; this Treehouse was special, Desmond was well into *Action Man* so we had a firefighter pole running straight through the middle of it. It was really just an old scaffolding pole but to me at that age, it was definitely a firefighter pole.

Oh my days, that pole was a stroke of genius; I could be my superhero Batman, I even pretended to be Tarzan sometimes so of course that pretense included Pam as cheetah the monkey. Once everyone was out, I would march her outside and push her literally to get up the tree and into the treehouse with me.

It was dangerous to get her up but not as dangerous as being indoors, we shouldn't be doing it really; exciting that's all I thought.

You don't think of dangers as a child now do you? I knew once my sister was up there that was it. I could play freely; unless I specifically asked her she wasn't going to move, just sit there and suck that thumb of hers staring into oblivion or at what I was doing. I swirled down that pole as many times as I could before my little hands would burn from the friction, talk about blisters ouch! I tried pulling my sleeves over my hands once but I flew down that pole a little too fast, wasn't keen on doing it like that again.

The only thing that could dull my excitement was watching Dad kill one of the chickens. They would screech when he came to the coup. I swear they knew one of them was for the chop, it was funny watching them dart left and right running Dad ragged and him pouncing trying to catch one. Dad was short and chunky in form so not very fast. When he did eventually get one oh dear, it was as though he was taking revenge.

"Mi ketch yu little backside," huffing and puffing, speaking under his breath.

Dad didn't really speak patois too well; he had his own unique American kind of slang, mixed up with the British and around the world phrases; when I think of it now although he said the right words a lot of it sounded really strange.

Holding the chicken firmly with both hands he would wring its neck. Poor thing didn't die straight away; instead, it ran bumping into things screeching. It's little neck bouncing off the side of its body still attached by a sinew horrible.

To think I ate that poor chicken after, mind you we knew better not to leave anything on our plates. If Dad knew we were in the tree house giggling at him chasing that chicken oh Lord!

When I think back to the time he caught us no, I was certain I didn't want a repetition of that I don't know who I felt sorrier for, me for enduring a severe beating or Pam to have to see it.

It all started off so pleasantly to that day, the type of day you could do just about anything in, not too hot and not too cold simply perfect, Pam didn't even put up a fuss when I took her away from the television.

"Come on Pam, look how nice it looks through the window! Let's go out and play in the treehouse."

"Iii wwant jjjuice fffirst." Pam stutters her words more when she's eager.

I fetched the juice quickly and she drank it just as quick, I washed and dried the cup straight away, we were not allowed to have anything before time, so I couldn't leave any clues and then we went out. The breeze was gentle like feathers it stroked our cheeks and arms.

I only had on my vest type tee-shirt with a hand me down pair of corduroy trousers on, the type with a crisscrossed strap to fasten, even one of the buttons was replaced with a pin.

Pam had her dungarees on too but hers were made out of cotton and she had her handkerchief stuffed into the front pocket. When Pam was in the mood to play I could stay with her forever.

Once at the Big Oak I went down on my knees to help Pam get on my shoulders,

"get on then, no not like that not a piggyback, you have to get on my shoulders we're going up the tree aren't we! Put one foot at a time don't worry I'll hold you, you can lean on the tree trunk."

She was scared to jump up to reach the first notch hold to get up the tree, the rest was really easy with all those low thick branches.

"Have you got it yet?"

"Gggot it now,"

"phew! That's good Cheetah."

I called her Cheetah so she would know what game we would be playing, I pushed her up the rest of the tree to ease her reach to each branch. Once at the opening to the treehouse I could relax she was out of danger therefore so was I.

We went in turned around and looked out, I called like Tarzan

"arh a arh a arh arh!"

That call made me feel invincible.

"Cheetah want a cuddle?"

"Ooo! Ooo! Ooo!"

Pam played along with anything I wanted her to once in that mood, she loved playing Cheetah too because I gave her lots of cuddles and tickled her belly. "Hah hah hah,"

"Cheetah stay now," that was me telling her I wanted to have some fun of my own.

My fun was always sliding down the pole, when I did that I became Batman my super hero and Pam became Robin.

The fun came to an abrupt end on that particular day, we got caught because we stayed out a little too long. I could hear water running into the back drain that meant Dad was back.

"Quick Pam come on, Oh God come on now,"

I couldn't have been happier that I was back in the tree and not in the garden, Pam wouldn't go down the pole though she was too scared, and we had to sneak in quick, what was I to do?...

As usual Pam was taking her time, I was scared stiff shaking as I went down first.

"Come on Pam please, Daddy's home, I'll hold your feet and put them on the branches, just hurry up."

She listened but I knew it was too late. On the ground I could see Daddy in the window, he didn't see us yet so I grabbed hold of Pam and pulled her to run, with only a few steps she fell, God forgive me but I just dragged her hoping she would get back up, but I scraped her knee in the process.

Dad heard her cry. "A weh de backside unnu doing outta back."'

Dads face was so scary to look at when vexed, through the window it was framed which makes this memory even more vivid. His voice penetrated through the crack of the window. I just couldn't look anymore, Pam was still crying and she had a big green bogey on her cheek that she wiped off with the back of her hand, she then held out that same hand to me.

"'Eeh yack" I said slipping my attention for a second but I held her hand anyway and we approached the back door to Dad.

He grabbed me by my Corduroy trouser strap and wacked me with the milk saucepan at the side of my head and neck. My head bounced back and forth but I didn't cry, it hurt like hell and I felt like I was under the bath water.

I turned to see him take Pam to one side and attentively clean her knee with Dettol on some cotton wool from the first aid kit. I watched and held my breath to try and silence my heart.

Pam's wound was so slight I could hardly see it once cleaned but that made no difference to Dad.

"See weh yu do to har, open de draw."

"No Daddy please Daddy please please,"

"mi seh open de draw or mi a go beat yu til yu open it."

The draw held a small piece of curtain wire about two foot long, I went to the draw shacking like a leaf, Pam looking rocking knowing what was coming sat quietly on the kitchen stool.

The sting of the wire across the back of my hands as I tried to protect my legs was so sharp I wet myself but he carried on and Pam rocked harder. I couldn't even cry it was as if I had no breath. When he finished he stripped off my lower garments right there leaving me in only my vest type top and marched me to the bathroom and stood over me whilst I washed my clothes out.

My hands were red raw wailed and swollen, Pam waited on that stool for me and when she saw me she offered me her thumb. I never got caught again but I still played in that treehouse. Daddy went on to make himself a cup of tea like nothing had occurred.

Usually he was back from God knows where, about a couple of hours after everyone else left. He must have been used to early mornings, always finding something to do pottering about.

Pam and I would be left in front of 'Watch with Mother' TV programme, that certainly wasn't right. Maybe Mom thought it was okay because our uncle was in the house or other people somewhere but we could have injured ourselves especially when Pam had one of her tantrums.

The pressure I felt when to me everyone had gone, and although I enjoyed being in charge. It was the play factor I liked not the caring bit. Talk about splitting hairs, great excitement and absolute fear all mixed up.

Television was a comfort blanket to Pam; I watched it sometimes but it was a bit too babyish for me what she liked. That's why at any given opportunity my preference was to take her outside.

Yeah, I was four or thereabout going on fourteen; must have been born with an enhanced aged brain I think because I can't think why I wasn't excited by those programmes like my sister.

Could it have been because we didn't really have many toys?

Mom was more into useful stuff; toys were a waste of money so I wasn't relating to its content or concept of play I guess.

We certainly didn't play like what they were displaying on those programmes as siblings; we just fought like 'Tom and Jerry.' Proper sibling rivalry.

Muffin the mule was so unrealistic with its clumping wooden legs, as for Andy Pandy well that was a clown in striped pajamas! I just didn't get it.

Now 'Batman' the cartoon character hero and the sixties television series, that was more up my street I could relate to that so that's what I liked to play as.

We as children, Mother and father gave us nicknames; 'Bebby' was Pam my baby sister as she was the last, up from me was Sarah, hers was 'Beafaren;' no, I didn't get that name either at the time, I thought it was because she was bereft, had lost something. Now I understand, poor sis, she was so skinny with a pop out belly, looking like one of those starving third world kids at death's door; maybe that's why she was given that name, she was always certainly sickly.

That bronchitis cough, terrible earaches, and those wobbly legs. She's registered disabled now, due to both her ears having bad hearing impairments her legs are fine now though thank heaven.

Jenna was next up; they called her 'Chookley,' it sounds like a chunky chocolate doesn't it? She was a bit chubbier than the rest of us, so I guess that's why. My other sister, Sheila, I won't ever know where the hell that one came from, 'Toady eye Jezebel' nothing wrong with her eyes at all.

Martha now hers was funny, 'Martha Gwarna,' she was always up to something, planning to go off somewhere, 'Wah gwarn' is a patois phrase for: what's going on. The funny thing is she did always have something up her sleeve a proper little gypsy, traveling everywhere. No real rooted feet, from Skegness to Saudi Arabia, yes really, we never know what's going on with Martha. How do we solve the problem with Martha? Find her a jolly good husband I say. Desmond he's was simple just Desi the Menice that's all.

My name aha! It was 'Batman cacaman.' Batman fine by me the other bit, I know weird right, but the tomboy in me relishes the fact that that's what Mom and Dad might have seen in me, a courageous fighter for justice or was it simply my over exaggerated imagination. They often said, 'caca fart... these strange wordings are all Jamaican Patois twang. Whenever they saw something extraordinary 'caca fart' was said or 'cooyah' so me being an extrovert I guess it was well suited then.

My bigger sisters always said, "Chu! yu too damn extra" and I was. They might have been slightly jealous perhaps! Blimey, I certainly was envious of them. I suppose Mom and Dad thinking I was responsible enough to watch my sister was some kind of endorsement of my character. (Of course, that's pure speculation).

They certainly saw the fighter in me though, because that's all I did.

Eleven months older that could hardly warrant me responsible enough to care for Pam now could it so I fought against doing it often even when I knew I wouldn't win I was only just handling myself. Gosh! What were they thinking? Who nowadays? In their right minds, I hasten to add, would leave a couple of children under five years old even if for just a few minutes?

When I had my own children, I could see the character personalities of my two kids. When I had the third with my second husband, he agreed that the names I'd chosen were suited. It was really easy to give our son one so Mom and Dad's nicknames for us must have held some significance.

Silly names mind you weren't they? They didn't stick of course only Jenna's really 'Chookley.' We just wouldn't grow out of using hers; I'm sure she had a complex over it as it meant chubby, I did over being called hooter because I had the biggest nose. We didn't mean to carry it on for forty plus years. We certainly didn't mean to use it for anything less than an endearing gesture of our childhood. Whenever we get together which I'm ashamed to admit it's very rare. We still use it, especially after a few glasses of plonk. Jenna poor thing, she's still the chubby one even after numerous trials of various dieting; did we all contribute to her settling herself into her nickname? Some of the names she calls herself; walrus, seal and bull sounds like she has to me. We were or I should say are, very self-critical.

I certainly still battle with, not necessarily the nickname 'Batman cacaman,' I still feel a sense of pride from that. No, it was from the effects of being left in a position of responsibility when I clearly wasn't anywhere near ready that I found difficult to shake off. Was it because I was given the nickname Batman? I know it made me push so hard to excel in things nobody offered or wanted to help me because they felt I didn't need it; the opposite was the real truth.

There is a lot to be said about treating you a certain way over a long period or giving you a nickname that to you isn't suitable. Obviously mine being Batman meant I was capable, could handle anything, a hero. If something did happen I could get myself out of it.

'Sticks and stones may break my bones but names can never hurt me.'

I beg to differ, some name-calling can hurt and scar very deeply indeed; called it often enough you also believe it.

Self-fulfilling prophecy perhaps? Names and labels can really hurt, my sisters used to pull on my nose and call it a hooter, it hurt so much that, I actually thought of having rhinoplasty once, until I saw what Michael Jackson did to his. It's not even that big, but they made it seem like it was huge and that's my point; It's always how we perceive something where the danger lies. You've seen my picture what do you think, should I have had the rhinoplasty?

CHAPTER TWO

THE FORMIDABLE MRS. CAMPBELL AND YVETTE

I started to say before that we were okay to play for a couple of hours before Mrs. Campbell came. Mother asked Mrs. Campbell to come and look after us in the day, but she could never get to us before 11 am.

She had her own things to do at home first, so I still had the responsibility of caring for Pam until she arrived.

Mrs. Campbell was a real and 'raw' Jamaican woman; Mom was also from Jamaica but unlike Mrs. Campbell Mother was very light skinned and looked like the Queen.

I might be wrong, actually I hope I am but I think my Mom was a bit of a snob, she must have been otherwise why did she try to talk posher when Mrs. Campbell came.

Good on her though Mrs. Campbell because she never did pay Mother any mind, I didn't at the time but now looking back I think Mrs Campbell was true to who she was beautifully authentic and unashamed of her roots. I certainly now understand a phrase she used in reference to the differences between house and field hands.

She was about the same height as Dad, definitely not as tall as Mom; her hair was always covered with different scarves, all brightly coloured. The dress sense she adopted was strange to me, not like my Mother's at all, more layers with odd shaping. I don't suppose she had much choice with our cold dampish climate. She wasn't long over from the sunshine parish of St. Catherine, Jamaica and the sun certainly didn't follow her.

It wasn't easy for her because she had not yet begun to mould into the English way, speaking to us in patois; was all she knew which was of course customary to her. Every now and then she would come out with the most bizarre phrases, but soon realised we had no idea what she was on about; we would continue therefore to do whatever she found irritating or dangerous because as far as we were concerned she was simply muttering to herself as per usual not to us.

The only thing she could do was to resort to her equivalent of the queen's English, which wasn't good and sounded even more bizarre. We really took a dislike to her from the onset.

When Dad came back we knew she wouldn't be far behind, so we needed to get back into the house without him seeing us. It was easy once he went near the coup; play time was well and truly over.

Once indoors I had a brilliant hiding place or so I thought, Mom and Dad had an enormous wardrobe that had a revolving section with mirrors. I would put my arms into a long heavy garment and close it up. I now became a second coat hanger; I thought that was simply perfect undercover spy work something Batman would be proud of!

What was the point though? When Pam would hide on the settee with cushions on her top-half only. Bless her, she thought if she couldn't see Mrs. Campbell, Mrs. Campbell couldn't see her, she then proceeded to tell and show her my whereabouts I could hear her from inside the wardrobe.

"shshshes iiin ttthere, cccan I havvve sssome jjjuice now?"

Pam would do anything to get more juice, clever enough to remember where I was though wasn't, she! I cannot say I was surprised really, considering I shouted at her to hide somewhere else.

"Go away! You can't hide in here with me, go and find your own hiding place."

Poor Pam, she hadn't a chance and served me right for being cruel.

"Cum out a dare yu little ginal yu, yu tink mi hav time fe chase yu, chu, you privalige house han pickenee yu will neva no boat fiel work, uhum yu lucki is a shame."

The minute we were both in Mrs. Campbell's clutches, she got that big old straw type bag of hers, and every kind of implement was in it. She took pride in laying out the contents, Bay Rum, cough mixture, more cough mixture, handkerchiefs, some crackers, an apple,

"oh see it here a dat mi want."

She then pulled out a rolled cloth containing a pair of knitting needles, didn't know they were that at the time.

"Nutting can beat dem fe part up yu hair good."

Then out came the combs.

"Ouch!"

She would chop you on your head if you so much as flinched,

"you're hurting," I would yelp,

"urting! Yu want mi fi give yu someting dat really urt?"

"No, Mrs. Campbell,"

"Shut up! yu too fresh," she would say continuing to rake away from root to tip just like Mommy. Never minding a tangle or two they were coming through regardless, thank goodness for the green pomade.

Mrs. Campbell abhorred procrastination; she got on with the job in hand and then moved on to the next. She had bills to pay and still two children of her own to bring over from Jamaica; I never heard her mention a husband.

She was always saying, "unnu hav it good, tru unnu nu no it yet,"

I understand her now of course. By the time Dad came inside; we would have our hair neatly combed, all the beds were made, the washing started, the big bar of green carbolic soap only a sliver of its former self overworked by the brutal hands of the determined to finish Mrs. Campbell. The fireplaces stocked and cleaned of loose ash; even the vegetables were washed and peeled ready for Dad to cook.

Mother worked you see, well that was the call; you came over to England to work there was no coming and waiting on the state handouts then.

Mother was twenty years Dad's junior but it didn't make a difference to them because he was more or less semi-retired and being a seaman before it gave him a good income.

So Mom had a comfortable start to married life she only really worked because she wanted to, I would want to be me and not just a Mommy too. He already had a home, enough funds aside and plenty of connections after renting out our rooms etcetera.

Dad was not one for sitting down too long however, he did work still on a crane in construction, but it wasn't every day and there were long spells of him not working at all. At those times he would do lots of odd jobs; decorating for others, grow vegetables to sell and keep us younger ones of course. It was okay because we still had a few pounds coming in from the lodgers' rents which Dad collected and put to various uses. Bit of an upside-down kind of family unit we were but it worked for us; well only financially.

Mrs. Campbell came in every weekday and I don't think we would have been able to manage without her, Dad certainly wouldn't have and I definitely couldn't. The time I had with Pam on my own was enough pressure, especially when she had a tantrum.

Sometimes, Mrs. Campbell would have to bring one of her own children with her; she was much older than me, her name was Yvette. She talked funny a bit like Mrs. Campbell but even quicker.

I picked up a great deal of, I suppose you could call it 'swagger' from Yvette I once tried to copy her walk.

"How come you walk like that?" I asked her, she replied

"mi havfe wok ard an farse so mi save up mi enargy wen mi wark."

I ended up walking a bit like a duck and she just laughed at me. Yvette showed me how to braid my sister's hair too now that was useful and it didn't take me very long before I was doing my own, what a relief that was; no more succumbing to the forceful hand of her Mother.

How come Yvette was so nice though? I remember my sister Sheila trying to show me how to braid. I pretended I didn't know how to, but I did. I pretended because I wanted the attention, I always wanted attention. With Yvette, I never had to fight for attention she was always giving me as much as I wanted, showing me things like words and numbers and talking to me, laughing with me and more importantly she helped me cope with Pam just by listening.

I think from her nature she was the eldest and I know at times I wished my older sisters were more like Yvette. I sensed, perhaps she never saw her Mother much either until she came to ours because she was always looking for approval.

She liked coming with her Mom to our house, and I kind of understood, the wanting to please her part. I did too with my Mom and Dad, maybe that's why I really liked her. She was also very aware that her Mother worked extremely hard always saying,

"mi mumma wok ard is a shame."

The irony of this is that years later, I became just like Mrs. Campbell for a long time, and my daughter, Yvette.

I said life can be funny, didn't I? How many of us look in the mirror later in years and say, "oh dear, I'm turning into my Mother."

Well, my Mother wasn't around at the impressionable stages in our lives due to, work first, then illness; certainly, never addressed any issues with us or sat us down to show and instruct; so for me, it was Mrs. Campbell.

Those Dirty Beige Trousers

I'm not the first and won't be the last to admit that as a child, we do not know what's best for us.

What we do know is only what we like, so at times we portray selfishness. Since I always had to look after my sister, my display of selfishness still involved her. I felt hard done by, but in truth, she was the making of me.

I believe that God instilled in me the skills to care and create, but in order for them to manifest, He had to place me in a position, along with challenging situations to have them enhanced. There's that hindsight stuff! If I only knew that then, It would have prevented a great deal of heartache and resentment.

Looking after Pam wasn't easy going; she had those tantrums and some of them were quite aggressive. She would hit me, and I wasn't much bigger than her so yes, it did hurt.

If it were one of my other sisters I would most definitely hit back. I never hit Pam back. I pushed her away but never did I hit her. We had good times and endearing moments, she would display some hilarious humour but there was a downside to that with her terrible stammer. When she got excited about something and was being descriptive and funny, it came out so you could never get the full essence of Pam's personality because she would put the breaks on when she couldn't control it, I think I was the only one that truly saw Pam for Pam.

Stammering hindered her terribly and made her frustrated. Pacifying her at those times was very difficult, to the point I had to endure the most bizarre of her habits, *ear sucking*, I'm telling you it was cringing. My little sister sucked her own thumb endlessly but wanted to suck my ear when really upset, yuck!

All slobbering saliva down my neck and the intensity of the sounds, like hearing the last bit of bath water going down the plug but amplifying that by ten! yeah exactly!

This pacifying was my nemesis, but I endured it. My caring nature was developing with every nasty slobbering suck. There was more in it for me this caring role and nature, I must say I did enjoy the power of it even whilst moaning how unfair it was.

Yvette taught me how to braid; so as my sister could sit for hours I had to allow her to 'rock' mind you, I could practice braiding her hair. I would comb it gently, that was easy because she had hair like our big sister, all silky only shorter.

Sometimes I'd plait the ends of the braids together to make a lace pattern effect, *check me out!* Oh was I getting creative or what?

So pleased with myself I had the audacity to say to Mrs. Campbell one day;

"Mrs. Campbell, I'm better than you at this."

What! You should have seen her suck-lemon face.

"Oh, so you think so do you, child."

Yvette stepped in and said, "yu rememba mumma is yu same one tell mi fe 'watch and learn,' yu nu tink seh she pick it up quick den."

Mrs. Campbell looked at her, "who tell yu fe farse In a mi bizaniz, yu tek tings mek joke, yu betta mine mi nu lambase yu behine."

Mrs. Campbell sucked her teeth harshly, "dyam pickeney dem." Wow, that patois could pack a punch.

Ah! Thanks Yvette, the point I missed; Mrs. Campbell was giving me and Pam 'Instructions' teaching us about respect, something missing in our lives.

Fear! Oh, we had fear down to a tee! Respect however, not really. Well I didn't; for that, even though at the time I didn't realise I certainly didn't like it much yet more people telling me what to do I'm forever grateful to them both. I was still quite selfish and cheeky; mind you, it took a great deal more than a one-off chastising to break me. I continued to take all the glory for myself,

"look what I did, doesn't this look better like that?"

Being an arrogant little brat didn't wash with Mrs. Campbell or Yvette for that matter. Soon they simply stopped responding to my beckoning trumpet blowing and kept making that sucking noise with their teeth.

It was all down to me wanting to be noticed simply that. Every one of my siblings got noticed for one thing or another, even if it was a naughty thing.

I was just the one looking after Pam and I felt overlooked, invisible.

Sarah with her bronchitis, bad ears, and skinny body, she got a whole lot of nurturing. She used to be the one sitting next to Dad if he decided to sit on the settee and not his armchair just for her, he'd cuddle her close and she'd be nestled in on his paunch belly, mmm! I had to watch all that and think I must really be ugly or bad, It's not as though she was really with the others; there was a good deal of time when it was me, her, and Pam. I think that's where it all started, Pam got seen, Sarah definitely did, so even though I was in the middle of them two it seems I was missed altogether.

Daddy nurturing Sarah, Daddy and Mommy telling me to watch Pam, me getting beatings because of not doing things right. In my case I was the thorn between two roses not the other way around.

Then there was Jenna, well, maybe that kind of attention I could do without, she and I definitely got the most beatings however, she was at least noticed.

Jenna and I were aesthetically similar in the body at that time and we took after our Dad's side more than Mother's, sort of rounder in features only she was chubbier than me. Sheila, she made herself noticed that's for sure, really confident she was and always playing the nurse.

Sheila, Sarah, Desmond and Pam were definitely Mother's side without any doubt, much straighter European features, they had Mother's nose; the rest of us Dad's, mine being the largest unfortunately. Martha was a straight fifty-fifty, we all had lovely hair but hers was the best and the longest. Martha and Desmond, being the first boy and girl, they did okay for themselves; got everything new for a start, so they couldn't complain.

Speaking of new stuff; I would have loved a few new things on my birthday, not just the hand me downs or something useful. Having a very nice cake was great though, Dad could make delicious cakes, brilliant in the kitchen he was, he could make something from nothing; a real talent.

I really don't understand how he could take time out to show off his cooking flare, but not find the time to give us advice; it's not as though he was illiterate far from it.

I accepted my *hand me down* gifts; it would always be what the others no longer wanted or couldn't fit into, all moth-eaten or threadbare. But they at least for that day, they made me feel like someone.

This was our status quo, and I just had to get creative; we certainly weren't the only family facing that. If I wanted to change something, I had to try it myself.

So, Pam became my experimental mannequin. I started by turning the clothes inside out and noticed that the fabric looked newer, hmm! Interesting, if only I knew how to sew or what sewing was.

One day, I got Pam to put on several blouses, no, not at the same time.

"Pam do you want to play a game with me?"

"Iii wwaant jjjuice fffirst."

Flipping heck she always wanted juice, she knew how to get her way that's for sure.

"Stand still for me then please you can finish your juice after, I need to put these on you, you'll look like a princess."

I placed elastic bands over the sleeves just in the middle of her forearm and pushed them up; this helped disguise the worn-out elbows. Once they were pushed up, I pulled some of the loose fabric down over the band. 'Wow! A bell sleeve,' now I never saw a fashion book, but I knew I liked the new shape. From then on, every blouse I wore, I would 'don' the elastic band bell look.

Poor Pam being my mannequin, I don't think she minded very much because I was giving her plenty of care and attention. But like I said to start with it was all for my own selfish benefit and it massaged my ego which I assure you needed no help whatsoever.

Mother had some really beautiful clothes, silk gowns and furs. Father too had wonderful pinstriped suits, matching cravats and cumber bands, braces with gold-looking clasping and fabulous shoes, both of them. He even had one of those watches with the chain that he would rest in his waistcoat pocket. I have to ask myself why then I got a load of the old tatt, there rested my anger and frustration.

Now, I have no idea where father came in line with his family whether he had all the leftovers or not but my Mother was the middle child I think.

Remember, I'm guessing as they didn't reveal a thing. We had an Aunt Ethel who was the eldest she was still in Jamaica and then Aunt Hilary I think. Then came Mother and Uncle Clinton I'm not sure if Aunt Mavis was the youngest; Uncle Clinton he was the uncle that lived with us, the so-called loner, forever the bachelor.

Uncle Clinton had a passion for beige or brown and smelt funny; he was always cooking liver and bacon and smoked Park Drive unfiltered cigarettes which made his fingertips and nails yellowish brown.

His second fix was his bags of sweets or was it what he could use them for?

Great big packets of them, Pear drops, Sherbet pips, and Lemon barley. I loved those Pear drops and he jolly well knew it.

What I wouldn't do for a Pear drop, don't even eat them now I can't even bear to eat a real Pear it's the smell. He did what he called a *swinging game.* Straight between his legs, he would swing us in such a manner ensuring our heads would stroke against his groin before he protruded through; he ensured we were all front facing too. I absolutely hated that game, now was that insight or instinct?!

Only God knows, it just didn't feel right to me, it made me nervous. Uncle Clinton had all these jokes and sayings, a real charmer and my brother Desmond found him fascinating a smooth operator. One of his repetitive jokes was, "you go on ahead and I'll hang around," playing it off with the tilt of his hat...

..."There you are, take a sweety..." He would say, after swinging us back and forth, bending down to my two foot something self, now uncomfortably paused in front of *those dirty beige trousers,* staring straight at a bulging zip sliding down from the built-up pressure behind it and those legs of his went up forever...

He was soon to go much further than a little swing between the legs. I didn't know at the time but me being uncomfortable was a sure sign and later, much later on in life it proved invaluable me knowing and sensing it was wrong of him as I was the only one willing to stand up to him.

One day many years later, Sheila and I sat at a coffee shop in Birmingham city centre. My sister confessed her suspicions to me, then Jenna and I concluded and confirmed she was correct in how she felt and what had occurred. Their memories needed clarification and on my detailed description of events they obtained it.

"What can you remember?" I asked her.

Her description was vague and brief but she was very upset and wanted to go to the police she was also thinking of our aunt as I had done for decades. When I revealed to her the licking of our groins and being turned over I knew I couldn't go any further as she couldn't handle it at all, Jenna, Sheila and I became closer because of what we shared and I promised to help any way I could.

I kept that promise when she was ready to hear the fullness of our trauma, and because of the revelations we decided between us to confront Uncle. I was there with my sister banging on his door one day ready to punch his lights out well. That is what I imagined myself doing, I know I wouldn't have done that but I imagined it for so long and wanted to so badly that when he wasn't in, holding all that back, well…

My husband was with us waiting in the car; what he must have been feeling for me, watching us walk towards Uncle's door, I'm not sure but it was deep and his face spoke volumes.

I returned to the car but because Sheila was with me both myself and my husband missed our opportunity to console each other in the moment. The opportunity to do so never really returned; I locked it away again but by the time we got back home after dropping Sheila off, he was also subdued not wanting to mention it in fear of hurting me.

The next thing I hear is that Uncle was very ill. Sheila later told me because she never got to Uncle she told Auntie Hilary who said she must find it in her heart to forgive, now that wasn't a denial was it?! I was sad to hear that he was ill and I don't know why to this very day. I do know I absolutely hated myself for having any form of emotion other than hatred toward him. It's possible I was feeling hurt for my Aunt Hilary I don't know but it wasn't a good phase. Later I heard he had died.

That was a seriously painful time for me; I was that close to getting the truth, to confronting him with my sisters backing, now I would never get my answers, never confront him, and I would have to continue as I was which was already bad enough.

Now just deal with it! That was me telling myself to shut up and carry on. My stagnant water now ran even deeper and I wasn't sure what current would steer it away.

That *'game'* he orchestrated, swinging us back and forth to hide the sick undertones of his subtle abuse was perpetrated on me, Pam, Jenna, and Sheila. Martha and Sarah were both spared the ordeal.

Sheila was much older; Mom and Dad not instructing us in life made us very naive indeed. If I felt odd about this so-called swinging game, even that is a poor choice of wording.

Why did the older ones allow it and seem to enjoy it?! They had no idea that's why, well they didn't seem to know when we were discussing it, it seemed they never knew for decades whereas I did.

My sisters came in the category of most people who have suffered abuse, having to come to terms with it later on in life. I can't tell which is the greater battle except they are both extremely hard to live with and face.

In hindsight, I think my sister Jenna may have felt slightly uncomfortable with it as a child by the way she held herself, crossing her arms constantly when he tickled her; her chubbier body would have given him greater pleasure she did seem to be tickled more often.

He was all hands on and in your space, the first person to give you a 'tickle.' When my kids were really young from babies to about three, I would do this 'raspberry blow' on their tummies.

It made them laugh intensely; I'm almost positive you would have or are doing it too; nothing like a chubby belly to blow, or a nice fat thigh to nibble, all above board and an act of a parent's natural love towards their offspring.

Uncle would do this too and after a thorough tickle, his motive however was far from natural; it was sinister.

His sick way of what I now realise was a 'feel up' would involve him diligently taking the time to pull our tights along with our panties down as low as he dared and blow right into our groin area.

My sisters laughed but I held my hands down to grip my tights from going too far, then wriggled like a baby not wanting their nappy changed; he thought it was because I was ticklish. Funny how I could do this when the others were around but when it was only Pam and me, he would go even further not just the raspberry blow but licking us in the groin too and wetting his finger to draw over our vaginas. I always froze. There's the truth, 'power in numbers.'

Two occasions of him going even further than that: one, was when he held me down over his knee after I came back from the toilet, and his excuse then was

"your skirt is up in your tights, let me fix it for you."

Over his knee, I felt my bottom exposed, and what I now know to be his penis being slapped over me several times; he said he was giving me *a little friendly tap.* He pulled my clothing back up and fixed my skirt, but couldn't do his zip back up fully because it was now bulging, the trousers worn those days were already too tight so you can imagine..

Actually don't! The image!

The second encounter; I was unfortunately front facing, he had Pear drops we were in his front room and he was sat down on a wide armchair by a long sideboard, he must have opened his zip at some point to take out his penis and was clever enough to disguise it in the cup of both hands.

I couldn't see it because he placed three pear drops in a line on the end of it. His two thumbs were covering the rest. It's so flipping obvious now I can see it for what it was, shit man if I could just go back and stop myself.

"See if you can get all of them off at the same time," he said.

I did along with his stiffened cock, as I did so he quickly let go of his hands as my mouth came close, that's why it felt strange underneath telling me that the long bit was just licorice. I almost choked and applauded myself for getting them all.

Although it was only one pull with my mouth to collect the sweets, I opened wide and took the full length of him. I can see myself sucking on those sweets all full in my mouth, the sounds they made and me licking my lips with satisfaction. Oh how he would have got off on that the evil sick swine.

They say abuse is often conducted by a family member our family member was Uncle Clinton. The only people that could have had an inclination or suspicion are all passed on now including my parents. Black culture honestly, so embedded in religion, tradition, and respect for elders all well and good that was rife, but shame; anything that would bring even a hint of it was swept under the carpet where bug and louse bread, an infestation of untold confession that later infects the inhibited with disease.

So today every one of us continues to live with the scarring of our stagnant waters; I hope none of my sisters' 'waters' are as deep or murky as mine and they find their way forward by whatever means they can.

We've taken various methods to overcome, diving into work each one of us something adopted from Mother. We all do care too, in some form or another whether in the health, counselling and prevention, or the medical treatment side. Putting others first helps a great deal, solving their issues however and not facing our own has its very low points indeed.

It's clear on our occasional liaisons that we all in some way or another still suffer low self-esteem.

Body issues mainly, but that's a very common factor amongst women. We're never satisfied. What can you do when it's impossible to remove your own head? You have to find a way to live with its contents and do your best to carry on don't you?!

Family foundations are our stem cells; it's what we grow from. Oh, we were a little unconventional, big house, lodgers in tow, a strange working pattern but it was new horizons for so many during that period; a new country with expectations that to everyone's surprise wasn't met.

CHAPTER THREE

MY UNCONVENTIONAL FAMILY

Father, he was born before the first Great War; in fact, even before the Titanic. 1909 was the year of his birth; an age like that I should I suppose have been speaking of my gran Dad. He was institutionally Americanised but had Victorian values.

The Americanism developed from him being in the American Naval forces and swearing allegiance to them, obviously from then on he would have had to do exactly as he was told no questions asked.

Dad's way of dealing with issues was harsh, emotionless even, as far as the rules were concerned. That's the only way he could get through as a black man I guess.

Some tough lessons passed through the generations of being owned came in handy as far as having enough resilience.

I'm not always convinced however that having a steel attitude serves us well. But like my kids would say to me, "your times were different mum."

Dad's genealogy proved a line of servitude, imagine all the rules through a day, with that history embedded he joins the navy. (Doesn't he look the part in the picture?)

I'm sure Dad's fore parents experienced some horrific encounters; only films like 'Roots' gave an inclination.

My Dad although not as severe, would have also endured a tremendous amount of racial segregation and black phobia amongst his peers on the ship. I hear it's still relevant today within the forces so most apparent then I'm sure. He was short as I've stated before and not very fast, so he may have found some of the training quite challenging. Oh, the mockery. He also had a dark complexion; this never went down well in those early eras. The darker you were the harsher the treatment.

I can tell you that that's a matter of opinion; as it certainly never applied if you were a woman, it didn't matter what shade you were the treatment would be horrendous. Being near white now that would have cost you your dignity, over and over again. I'm certain you don't need me to be graphical.

Dad may not have been considered aesthetically naval in height or physique the damn cheek of them. Okay to call for help from the commonwealth as they pleased; but then treat those that came to their aid like lepers, despicable.

The same uniform was the only unification; Dad most likely would have endured the worst bunk, the harshest of prejudices; he however thank goodness ended up being the cook, probably because he couldn't quite meet the physical necessity so there were no leftovers of food for Dad.

Everyone had to be able to swim and Dad was an excellent swimmer. This excellence saved his life.

The ship S.S. Lucrecia was the third one that was torpedoed during the war this was Dad's last ship but he was on all three. Yet again, Dad was one of the lucky survivors. (There are some references at the end of this chapter and some documentation.)

It must have been a very traumatic period. What he witnessed would have stayed with him as with others until they passed away. You only hear the stories don't you? close to the remembrance service.

What always hurt me when viewing these was the lack of reference to the black servicemen and they were so many. Finally in 2017 almost a century after the First World War and over seven decades after the second, the recognition came.

My poor Dad never got to see it; it's such a shame as he made numerous attempts to rescue his fellow seamen. He was such a strong swimmer, so he was able to sustain the cold and the current. It's a great pity it wasn't all documented.

I know he was given his service medals for the accord, and there was also a letter from Downing Street that's about it. I can see now why Dad had a picture of Sir Winston Churchill in our hallway something my Mother never really approved of.

All members of our family now have copies of the documentation to that said encounter and we also have a print of Dad's medals. My brother however has the actual items as he too joined the Navy eventually.

Beside this strict brutal no compromises side of Dad, there was a homely house husband who would sit and iron all the clothes for hours, cook large pots of seasoned rice, stew peas with oxtail or some other hideous form of offal, Saturday soup and Sunday roasts.

Dad's Saturday Soup

After the chosen veg were peeled, chopped and washed clean, my Dad would set this scene, window cracked to let out steam he would put a pot of water to boil, take out of the fridge some left over lamb neck or chicken back from foil, lift the pot lid and dash them in.

Next, he'll wash his hands off with a piece of lime then add the chopped leek, scallion, garlic and Thyme. All this was to flavour the meat, he would often taste the sauce as a treat.

Next the hard food would go in, the yam, green banana, carrot and pumpkin, lift the lid and dash them in.

When the hard food was part done, the softer food was next to come, a scotch bonnet, potato, sweet potato, and cho cho all to blend into the meat bone marrow.

Then came the best part, I watched my Dad dance and prance singing this tune. *'Mix some flour salt and water knead a dough until it can't be tighter. Some like a sausage some like a plum but roll and roll until the dough is done,'*

Then he'll lift the lid and dash them in, I'm telling you that scene really was the best thing.

He enjoyed cooking with the harvest of his own labour; he had growing things down to a fine art, rotating various vegetables to get the best produce as well as breeding those chickens. I try to imagine what my Dad would have been like as a child and what he may have witnessed. Workhouse conditions maybe! But unlikely in St Lucia. He would have worked hard no doubt about that, plenty of chores to do and he would have seen and had a lot of beatings I expect. What I'm unsure of as he and Mother never declared a thing, is his living conditions.

We were certainly not allowed to make a mess and play freely unless we were outside. Father was so very neat, possibly the navy training come to think; or was it because he never had much therefore valued every item, it doesn't matter as it kept us in good stead.

Now Mother please forgive me; I shouldn't speak ill of her especially as she has passed on. But my Mother wow! She was hard as nails and so uncompromising. She was near white remember that says it all in my book and looked very much like our Queen Elizabeth, even wore her hair the same way I don't know whether she thought that would help her get by in life or what. We never met our grandparents on either side, so I'm none the wiser to know if any of them were full white. If that were the case then some unsavory carrying on occurred, which could explain Mother's icy approaches at times.

The history passed down to her would have been difficult to hear. Her favorite saying to us was, "you made your bed now lie in it." Oh she always looked like thunder when she said that. She must have had it said to her many times because she really wanted us to know, if you made a mistake nobody would be willing to help you.

Or they just couldn't. *Poor Mother*, I realise I keep saying that but so much of what she said or didn't say, do or didn't do just spells such fear and hardship to me. I don't know what they experienced but they did have that stiff upper lip.

They were so stiff that we barely got a hug, teaching us to be able to take any kind of setback, any kind of knocks, any kind of abuse, anything life would throw. I suppose they truly wanted us to be ready and able; as we practically dragged ourselves up and those beatings. Things like finding out about our menstrual cycle, my God we found that out in the most embarrassing of ways that's for sure.

And because my older sisters weren't told they didn't tell us younger ones either.

How was I supposed to know how a tampon went in! I just wedged it between my legs and only took a few steps then out it came, dropping on the floor scarlet. I soon found my way out of that, covering it quickly with my foot then sticking it in my shoe.

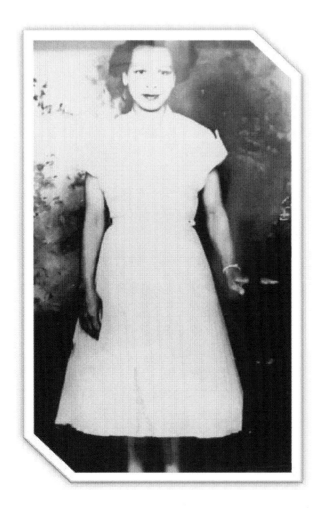

Wish I wore tights; that day taught me alright for not taking the big pad. Martha said, "Oh you got blood coming, it's okay take this with you and put another one on now."

I should have taken it but that belt and those hooks, it looked like a stuffed cricket sock. I used some toilet paper and went to school it was very uncomfortable so I asked my friend if she had anything and she did, I took the tampon from my friend instead, and was so delighted by its size in comparison it really did looked like it was meant to wedge in between my legs, she obviously thought I knew what to do with it.

Mistakes, oh yes, plenty, not a stitch of guidance, the only thing we were taught was complete and utter independence.

Right this very second, I'm welling up because we got through okay and none of us have ended up in an institution because of mental health issues. Well, only Pam, but that's not like a hospital; it's more a homely place with her own quarters and communal areas that she can seek assistance from, and I for that matter.

Thank goodness for 'Mencap.' We are not dependant on drugs or alcohol; we are all regular girl and boy next door kind of folk. Apart from a short spell of counselling for myself, I can't speak for the others we've all done Okay.

We are all in our fifties and sixties now, and the effects of our childhood did bare some lasting scars however, Uncle bloody Clinton for instance and we never got around to sharing a great Christmas with lots of present exchanges.

We never really had a good start to it that's why; we just about send a card, took years after we all went our separate ways to even hug one another. Not surprisingly that some of the family are now Jehovah's witnesses not much of a celebration to miss, not that they don't take their faith seriously because they certainly do, very God orientated we are.

Apart from the best real six-foot tree with so much tinsel and coloured lights it was hard to see any green unless it was shedding on the floor. Our Christmases were flat.

I remember one Christmas, Dad got out his 'smoking jacket,' burgundy velvet with a paisley collar and a rope belt it was. He put it on and took a big fat cigar from the sideboard. Dad usually smoked a pipe; it was only special occasions that he would (don) the cigar. So the scene is set, he is dressed for the occasion, he sits on the most comfortable chair; Dads always get the best chair don't they? He spreads himself out like a huge bear and begins to puff and pull as he lights it.

Ahh!

Big smoke rings appear in the room. I quite liked the smell; it made me feel calm and a bit sleepy. He would only ever smoke half at a time, though never all.

The bad part of this comforting scene was him calling me to proceed to do his corns and bunions; a chiropodist at four years old, well an apprentice in the making at least. Oh boy, poor little me, the smell of the Swan vesta matchbox used as a file on his toenails like a burnt saucepan it was and the dust went straight up my nose; more cigar smoke please.

Can you imagine a size nine-foot in my little hands? Not only heavy but it was also like filing the barnacles from the bottom of a kayak; Dad's feet saw harsh times that's for sure and they needed regular treatment because of his diabetes. I wonder how he coped during his naval days! Things were so different; regulating his sugar levels, taking his insulin, it's a wonder he passed the medical at all.

So much we did as children especially me, wouldn't be allowed today, then again.

Knowing Mom and Dad everything was a secret so we would still be doing it I suppose.

" You betta keep quiet, don't tell anybody, especially at school, dem will take you weh" a regular phrase Mom would say in patois.

She was right of course, if social services knew how much we were doing we would surely have been split up and fostered out when the going got tough; luckily it never came to fruition.

When both feet were done, Dad would do some magic tricks with money and bottle tops that was a bit of our Dad's humourous playful side. I think that as a child he and all children in Dad's era would have had to invent their own games. Dad was very imaginative; I know I get that from him, thanks Dad you did at least give me something.

When we had our dinner we got to open the one gift of a new board game. The room would be full of presents of coloured Christmas wrapping paper, and all of us in our best clothes, the smell of the Christmas dinner wafting through making us hungry.

Ludo was that years board game but only four can play at a time.

"I'm being blue,"

"green,"

"I'm red then,"
"yeah you would be" said Martha to Sheila,

"ahh shut up you."

"So I'm yellow then," said Sarah.

Pam and I simply watched and learnt. They soon got fed up playing because one or more of them would try to cheat. Mom only bought what was useful, wouldn't waste money on toys which is what we really wanted. Ludo was in between a toy and game. So that was okay.

We then opened up our wrapped items of usual pyjamas socks and knickers. Watching this, Dad would get nice and relaxed, re-light the other half of the cigar and puff away, all that was missing; the all-important western on the television but this was Christmas; the television programme this time would be 'The Wizard of Oz' it was our turn for the treat.

It's not long since they stopped showing that on Christmas Day. It still comes on within the twelve days however, perhaps now on one of those international channels, the child within me feels the warmth from it still because that was the times we all sang the songs together rocking on the settee, Martha was great at mimicking the wicked witch of the west.

So, Christmas was mediocre, what a shame you may feel. I don't know; the jury's out on that with me.
I've never taken anything in life for granted, did Christmas teach me that?

Mrs. Campbell and Yvette, or was it those unforgivable threadbare clothes and worn out shoes? It doesn't really matter because I certainly needed an attitude of that nature to get through my life.

The winters were so long and cold but they were kind of bonding times because it was freezing outside, not much play to be had. I told you we had sash windows; they were suited to the structure of the house.

It was nice when some of the stainings on the glass showed beautiful reflections in the low winter sunlight, but the frost used to creep through somehow and leave these sparkling spiraling shapes up the window that sucked Mother's lace curtains stuck like a sticky lizard's tongue.

The shapes were so mesmerising that I'd look at them for hours. Mind you, there wasn't an awful lot going on. If we weren't all sat on the sofa singing to ourselves. Two of our favourite songs were 'she'll be coming around the mountain,' and 'there was an old woman who swallowed a fly.'

It was great how we would take it in turns to start so the song went on forever, so comforting singing as we were watching the fire crackling and bits of embers falling in the grate. If we weren't singing we were in different parts of the house doing our own thing to entertain our minds.

One of my games was to count the tiles; now I couldn't count past fourteen or so. I knew up to twenty but got them a bit muddled up. The tiles were black and white, so it made me a little bit dizzy.

I remember quite liking that feeling, then falling on the floor, weird child. Since there wasn't much to do, Mom or Dad would allow a good deal more television, more 'Batman and Robin' 'The Saint,' and I think the 'Bond' movies besides all those westerns.

I can see myself now shadow punching and kicking making silly gun noises. If I had the brief chance to straddle the sofa whilst Dad went to the loo, I'd be the coolest cowboy in the land.

At Last I Get to Go to School

We spent another year or so in the big house, and within that period came school. I was so excited to finally get my chance; no more looking after Pam. I'm not being horrible; I wanted some time for myself, I was eager to learn, that's all. Yvette showed me stuff, helped me with my counting and how to write my name, I wanted to get to school so I could explore.

Sure, I was going to miss the Treehouse, even the games I'd play indoors, especially my experiments on Pam. The fact I was beginning to exhaust that shows it was time for new adventures and surroundings. The furthest I ever went from the house was into the garden or along a wall a little way down the road to steal some crab apples from the neighbour's tree.

Unless it was the doctor's surgery or being taken somewhere in the car I was now going to go all the way to school; I couldn't wait.

There just had to be something though didn't there to yet again burst my bubble. I wasn't getting any nice new clothes. Oh no not me, back then we didn't have to wear school uniforms to infant school anyway.
I had to endure bad clothes all my school life; there's a lot to be said about every pupil having a uniform even if it was a bit out of sorts, it was at least the same.

Mother tried a few of Jenna's on me first as she got too big for quite a lot of hers. Then some of Sarah's, all in all I had a mixture; some old corduroy dungarees, a blue and a brown one. I already had enough shirts although rough around the collars and two skirts. I ended up with mostly Jenna's stuff; Sarah's was a bit too snug so then Mother said,

"I will put these aside, Pam can have them,"

What! Was Pam going to school the same time as me?

Phew! No, not just yet, I had a good year first, but the fear I predicted came to fruition alright when she did eventually begin school.

My whole new secure world fell apart and my personality was hindered. In fact, it almost changed completely. I was established in music and Mrs. Rudder she was the music teacher said I had promise, anything creative really, I shone.

That early start with Yvette, the counting and writing of my name helped a great deal because It made me feel confident, I was flying.

Walking to school was great, seeing lots of other kids all in their smart clothes, my keen eye observing what they wore with what, the colours, even the way the black kids had their hair, I was taking it all in. It didn't matter when the others went slightly ahead, I quickly knew where I was going.

The year passed speedily; I loved school that year, and it wasn't until year three before I felt that connection again. That was due to Pam starting and us having to move to a new house.

When the time came for Pam to come also, I knew the ball and chain would soon again be affixed to me and the others would carry on as they always did; they never took their share with her care really, it was always down to me.

I pulled the gloomiest face when Mom was getting her ready to start.

"A weh wrong wid yu, yu favar soar puss?"

"I'm going to be late,"

"yu nar go late, yu nar go by yuself mi a drive!"

I should have already gone but I was kept behind. Sarah, Jenna, and Sheila were going in after lunch because it was a day for new starters.

Martha and Desmond were already in secondary school, so they left much earlier. I thought this was so unbelievably unfair was I never able to be rid of her?

I had to go with Pam a couple of times, the only good thing about it was indeed that we went to school in the car. Our car was a big car, silver in colour with large red leather seats.

The back seat was like a sofa; when Mother drove, Pam and I would slide from side to side as she turned the corners, no seat belts in those days. We would giggle as we fell into each other's laps pending a right or left turn.

We felt very important arriving at the school gates because nobody else came in a car, some teachers but not all of them; obviously before I walked when I went with my sisters, this was purely for Pam's benefit certainly not mine.

After the initial staring us down coming out from the car, we walked in, Pam holding unto my skirt with one hand whilst the other was to her face with her thumb in her mouth. I didn't hold onto Mother, didn't feel the need to, as I'd been there before, in fact Mother brought unnecessary attention really.

I remember the corridors seemed very long, and they also smelt like varnish which I quite liked. It reminded me of home, our banisters. With the familiarity of my new taste of freedom, I began to relax. Soon I'll be in my class and Pam would just have to get used to things on her own, I thought.

First, we were shown into the assembly hall. This was the place we attended each morning, it had a very odd-looking floor a bit like bricks but wooden and a really strong smell of polish.

There were also enormous windows with thick velvet blue curtains and tie backs you could easily swing on.

It was the stage I kept looking at though, strangely drawn to it like a powerful magnet; it held precedence and I liked it.

The next stop was the classrooms wow! The first time I saw them I thought *"I'm free*! Finally I get to be apart from Pam; this might not be too bad after all."

In the classroom there were small wooden desks each with its own lid and little wooden chair on top, I was asked to try one out when I came

"oh! Okay," I said swiftly when asked.

The teacher placed the chair on the floor for me and I sat on it,

"open the desk" she said, so I did.

I lifted the wooden lid, and inside there was a blue book of lined paper, next to it lay a ruler and a fat HB pencil with its own eraser on the end.

"Get used to opening and closing the desk young lady you will be doing that for a whole year in here."

"What's this hole for miss lady?" I pointed at the inkwell,

"I'm Miss. Grantham don't worry about that, we don't use that anymore, It was to hold all the ink to dip the quill; pens used to be made from feathers,"
She then realised I hadn't a clue about what she meant by my facial expression, so she just smiled and said

"shall we move on?"

Miss. Grantham was posh looking, hair up in a tight bun and she wore a pearl necklace with matching earrings, I saw Mother looking at them and I knew she was thinking I got some like that only bigger.

I got up off the chair walked over to the blackboard to examine the funny looking block eraser; she put the lid down and the chair back on top of the desk then walked over to me and took my hand, her hand felt like a pillow so soft and warm, my tummy felt funny, butterflies of excitement filled me up and suddenly I felt myself jumping and giggling; I soon stopped embarrassed looking up at the teacher trying to be grown up so I let go of her hand and wondered back over to Mom.

I wondered then if Pam would feel the same as I did and find school as exciting as me. That would be so great; Pam was always on my mind maybe then she might just be strong enough to leave me alone and do some things by herself; I so wanted my freedom.

I snapped back to reality it was Pam's first time now not mine, I would often just dream away; it was because Pam nudged then looked at me and smiled. She wanted my reaction if I liked it so would she.

I was smiling for something quite different; my thoughts were of my escape from her. I wanted my little world here at school to continue, on the same path as before but get even more exciting, it was to be far from that.

Pam would take her own pace and I would have to tread with her.

This first day didn't last long for Pam as it was only an induction and Mother stayed with her throughout. After the classrooms I was allowed to stay in mine as usual, so Mom and Pam went to meet her teacher, oh no! Pam looked back at me and I thought she's beginning to panic, there's that look. After shaking hands and an exchange of words they were then told when to return. That look on Pam face troubled me, *I've lost all this* I thought, *I just know I have.*

The next day Pam again came with Mom but this time she had to stay until 1 pm. Mother couldn't stay that long, so she went off thinking Pam would be fine after the induction went so well, ha yeah right, Mommy didn't see Pam's face did she, but I did. Pam went to her classroom after an assembly of hymns and announcements; we always sang the National Anthem and said the Lord's Prayer then. Would Pam stop looking around for me? No, she wouldn't, fidgeting whilst we were cross-legged on the floor. I just knew something would go wrong, she wasn't settling at all.

In my classroom things went as I expected to start with. I opened my desk and took out my blue-covered book, drew my margin, wrote the date as seen on the blackboard. I began what was instructed of us and listened for the teacher's next request. About half an hour passed before there was a knock on the door, the teacher just finished saying to me,

"Jannette, how are you getting on?"

She looked down and saw I'd written my name, the date, and had a very straight margin. I had almost finished the work on the board.

"That's beautiful work," said Mrs. Ashcroft, "I can see you've had an early start on everyone."

My head exploded, and I felt myself going hot, what was this feeling? Didn't care, I liked it.

More please, I want lots more of this I thought.

Mrs. Ashcroft wasn't at all like my first-year teacher Miss Grantham, Mrs. Ashcroft was stern, she reminded me of Mother so when she gave me praise it was like receiving a huge hug from Mom and Dad.

Alas, praise was not what I got more of, I got more of Pam instead. The teacher that knocked came in, asked Mrs. Ashcroft to come and then they both stood outside the door chatting for a few minutes.

Mrs Ashcroft came back inside, and I was summoned.

"Quiet everyone I won't be long, I'm taking Jannette to see her sister."

The other teacher stepped in to make sure the other kids were safe. I realise now she must have been the secretary. I can't tell you how disappointed I was that I had to leave my class and my work.

So this is going to be my new experience in school!

I thought, *I knew it I just knew it after seeing that look on Pam's face,* why oh, why was I even surprised?
Pam took away my home life choices and she would do it here too.

Yvette filled my head, I did and could do so much more of the things I wanted with her. She was funny, clever, and never once did Pam get in the way of anything new shown to me when Yvette was around. Mrs. Campbell saw to that, never for a minute would I have thought I would feel a bereavement for both her and Mrs. Campbell.

I stayed with Pam through two lessons, one of which was only playtime, but I missed my reading time on the mat, one of my favorite things about the school. I was stuck in that medical room with her. Lunchtime came soon enough, when she was collected by Mother.

Soon she'd be back home, Dad would have to stop his gardening or pause his plans to garden, to stop and watch Pam. Now that wouldn't have been very nice for her no interaction that's for sure just plonked in front of the television, at least when I did it, I'd give her a choice of what to watch and have a little chat with her.

I know he was always pleased when I was around because after she started school properly, we removed our school clothes to put our house ones on, I made sure I put the television on for Pam.

My first responsibility was Pam, then I watched Dad in the garden, I did everything to please my Daddy. I watched him pulling out marrows as big as my leg, cutting cabbage heads and shaking off potatoes,

"good price for these, those are bruised, so that's for us," and so on he would mutter under his breath always mumbling he was.

He didn't mind me watching, but would say,

"make yourself useful and fetch some twine from the barrel, oh, and get some newspaper from the shed."

The newspaper was for wrapping; if he was feeling good about the produce I got to wrap and pack the tomatoes. They were always picked just a bit early then wrapped in the newspaper and placed in a drawer for ripening off; Dad said they kept firm that way.

That Thursday and Friday with Pam spoiling my school days planted a venomous seed in me, yes another flipping virus; the seed of fear. It weakened the real me even more and ignited my bossy boots characteristics.

It was sheer survival after that, life got even more tough. The weekends were sameness, Mom and Dad were around more but they went out sometimes on the Saturday. You should have seen the clothes they wore, so regal, absolutely beautiful, like a prince and princess.

The Ukinamis were in too because you could hear them pottering about upstairs. I think they attended church on Saturdays. Then there was Uncle Clinton who came and ate with us on the Sunday's.

Going back to school, however was the only thing on my mind, surviving a whole week of school with Pam in tow and she would be attending all day like the rest of us. It was only a couple of hours before I was interrupted at her induction, how the hell was I going to get through a whole day a whole flipping week?!

The rest of that weekend passed in a flash and the closer the the time for school came, the more dread I felt. The routine started, shoes were polished, clothes were sorted and put in little piles after being checked for size or repairs; then it was the night before after a long day of church. Could I sleep?

It was Monday and the beginning of the school week proper; there was to be no more driving us to school. Mother seemed to believe two times was enough to settle Pam, uhmm! I'm five that's all and Pam is four but my Mommy seems to think that's okay to allow us to walk!

It was only a straight road mind you, a bit winding as you started to get up the hill and there was a junction to cross, thank goodness there was a lollipop attendant. When I used to go with my sisters they got ahead of me a bit sometimes but at least I could still see them. I told you didn't I! That Mom and Dad taught us how to be completely independent.

Walking to school with Pam was a chore she walked too slow she was always taking her own sweet time. Our siblings didn't wait, they were not going to be late, late meant Mr. Stanly. There I was worrying about Pam, she could panic, have a tantrum meltdown. Boy oh boy, did she make it difficult! I got all hot and bothered watching the image of my sisters ahead of me get smaller and smaller as I dragged her almost all the way to school.

Being a September child, I was of course one of the oldest in my year, as Pam was an August child and born on the 30th at that, she was one if not, the youngest. A whole year difference would have been hard enough to catch up in our development but with Pam being autistic too, it proved quite an ordeal for us both.

I'm not entirely sure why it felt different this year but it did. The playground seemed vast and in every corner there were children gathered in various cliques. There were some very big kids like Yvette, some even bigger. I guess I was looking at it differently because I was viewing it as Pam may see it. I was no longer just thinking of myself. My freedom had ceased and I was kind of prepared for that. I could see now why the older pupils were absent from school when we had our induction periods. If last year, I had seen school the way I now saw it, I might have been very nervous myself.

My first time though and for that whole year I was so overly eager to get away from Pam and the responsibilities of home.

I would have seen anything through rose-coloured spectacles. Before, I ogled each area with my curious mind and felt nothing but sheer excitement, now I couldn't wait for the bell to ring. Phew! What an absolute relief it was to hear that sweet sound 'dingalingaling'.

"Get in line now children, quick as you can," said the playground attendant as she clapped her hands together chauffeuring all us kids to our designated lines.

"All you new pupils, do you remember which class lines you were to go into?" "Just look for your class teacher, she will remember you."

I found my teacher, she had the same stern look as Mrs Campbell so easy to spot. Pam followed, "no I said, you need to go to the teacher you had when we came with Mommy remember.'

As I felt the difference Pam did too, all those big pupils scared her, it's funny how I never even noticed them before. It wasn't happening today, she wasn't going to cope like she did on her induction, although there was a little blip on that day.

It wasn't going to be nice, I felt that my new exciting world was crumbling, she wasn't going anywhere without me. That ball and chain fastened tightly as she clung to me, I tried to ease her away gently saying, "it's okay, it's nice here; look I'm smiling, I like it, so you will, too won't you?"

I felt her start to fidget, oh no! When Pam fidgeted trouble came. She was about to panic; this was not going to look good for either of us.

Soon enough her teacher spotted her and came over phew! I sighed with relief as attention was building, the eyes on us felt uncomfortably invasive.

"Come on dear, this way," the teacher held out her hand to Pam.

Pam looked at the teacher's hand like it was a foreign object leaning in closer she looked straight at me as if I was sending her to jail and then she started,

"I'm with Jannette," but it didn't come out like that, it was the worst case of her stammering ever and everyone heard her. Stare, stare, everywhere, me, I just wanted to go home the sanctuary of school was gone. Be careful what you wish for, this wasn't the kind of noticing I wanted at all. The classes were hurried into school and we were taken to one side,

"I suppose you could come with us, again! I thought, just until she settles." said the teacher.

What else! Is what I was thinking, *you don't know Pam.* I wanted to go home so badly I've never wanted to do that before, why can't it just be about me for once.

"Miss," I braved the words, "I have other sisters too, can you get one of them, so I can go to my class? Or can I go home now? She can stay here, and I can walk by myself."

The teacher looked puzzled, I knew I said something I shouldn't, Mother's words rang deep in my head, "don't tell them anything at school, they will take you away."

Quickly, I reverted, "I can walk by myself because I'm a big girl now…"

The teacher's face softened. I wiped my sweaty palms against my skirt and then I held her hand and Pam's tighter feeling a bit scared, did she believe me? Were we now being taken away? Off we went, my knees went weak.

She took us to the medical room and the very nice nurse was in there, "oh dear, casualties already?" she said.

"No, this one," pointing at Pam.
"She's just a little nervous could you keep them here until the first break?"

"It's okay," she said "I've had them both here before, they'll be fine in here with me." Referring to the time I was called out of my class because Pam wasn't settled.

"I'm not nervous miss, can I go then?"

I felt back in control. The nurse looked at the teacher and the teacher at her, but they didn't look at me, *what's this about*? I thought!

Mrs. Campbell and Yvette did this 'looking stuff' when they wanted to ignore me. School wasn't making a difference to my life after all. Pam's presence had crushed it, smashed it up just like everything else, Pam, Pam, Pam. One year that's all I had to myself, one lousy year, I loved it. So now I was absolutely screaming inside.

At least twice a week I would find myself being taken out of my classes to sit in the medical room with Pam, at school with Pam, at home with Pam, Pam, Pam, Pam. The only saving grace was the huge box of dressing up clothes and toys so my imagination developed somewhat. There were books too, Peter and Jane with lots of pictures of family stuff and adventures, I tried to read them but couldn't properly, so I made my own stories up from the pictures.

I was good making up stories and would settle Pam with them, no choice really, as the nurse had no time to teach or read to us which was my favourite thing.

She was always doing other stuff. When someone was brought in to her with a grazed knee or hurt somewhere, I'd watch her administer the care.

How her face softened and her voice calmed, even her eyes looked different, interesting.

There was a nurse uniform in the box, I would mimic what she did with the pupil with Pam as my patient. It felt good to be in control again, it didn't stop me wanting to go back to my own class though. Nevertheless it was still, far better than being at home. I didn't try to walk off, I felt some relief as anything was better than home really.

Uncle Clinton hung around in the day sometimes you see, spoiling everything. It wasn't just the things that he did, or the way he made me feel. Even when just his name was mentioned, I would visualise those dirty beige trousers of his and that bulging zip, especially since I had that line of Pear drops. That memory was a parasite.

Why was it always after Mrs. Campbell and Yvette went home?

I didn't want to play with him, I could look after Pam and myself fine, she was safer with me on my own. We weren't safe around him that's for sure, we didn't need him thank you very much.

I bloody hated it when Mrs Campbell had to go and Daddy was too long coming home. It was as if he could smell his chance to have some 'sugar'.

The damn lanky long foot stinking old goat with him nasty finga dem chu! I certainly didn't want his liver and bacon and no more pear drops not at all.

If I had to swing through those lanky ladder legs ever again, take anymore balancing Pear drops, I was just going to have to play up and get into trouble, I thought. I'd rather get a beating of all beatings, the kind that made me pass water, even a good chop in the head from Mrs Campbell with the comb, anything... but play with Uncle Clinton. That's how desperate and uncomfortably fearful he made me feel, because the beatings were tortuous...

Oh, I didn't feel in control around him I had to protect Pam as well as look out for myself. I was responsible. Uncle took away my control, instantly and gave me the creeps in exchange. I really didn't understand why it made me feel powerless. My heart would become so rapid and I felt frozen; such a horrible feeling. Could it be any worse?

Yes, it could, besides me having nightmares about Uncle and all the new changes in school due to Pam being the way she was; we were about to move to a new house, the confusions would now intensify.

We had no idea we were leaving. Lodgers always came and went so nothing unusual in seeing them go. This time however, Mom and Dad were wrapping everything in newspapers and they began to argue like the lodgers, they were very short with one another and sharp with us.
You wouldn't think we could be left to our own devices anymore that it was already but we were, and now the 'Tom and Jerry' interactions between us siblings manifested, big time.

One good thing, Uncle Clinton had to go too!

When I look back at those times and think of the strength my father would have had during the war. Why didn't he put Uncle in his place? Dad swam in a sea through burning oil and more. Dad should have done to Uncle what he did to the chicken, wring his stinking neck off! He couldn't have known that his daughters were subjected to sexual abuse. We cannot get any of that settled now, it is the ultimate unanswered question. I wish I could.

Here are some of my father's documents and medals, although not very clear. If you use a magnifying glass, maybe you can read the account of his survival.

My father's service medals

My father's service documents

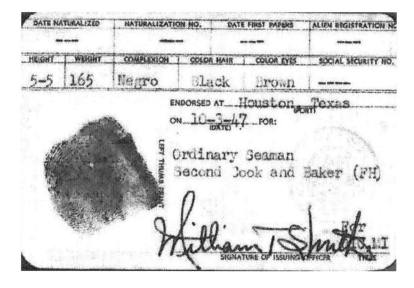

My father's short acknowledgment letter

UNITED STATES COAST GUARD

ADDRESS REPLY TO:
COMMANDANT
U. S. COAST GUARD
HEADQUARTERS
WASHINGTON 25, D. C.

18 October, 1949
MVP (D)
Z-571305

Mr. Augustine Joseph
Parkieten Bos.
No. 23 B. D 4
Aruba, Netherlands West Indies

Dear Sir:

Receipt is acknowledged of your letter of 10 September, 1949 concerning
duplicate certificates of discharge covering your service on the
SS FLAGSTAFF VICTORY and SS CHALMETTE. You state that you failed to
receive a reply to your letter of 17 May, 1949.

A copy of our reply to your letter of 17 May, 1949, addressed to you in
care of the SS LA BREA HILLS is inclosed for your information. As stated
in the third paragraph of the inclosed letter it will be necessary for you,
when you return to the United States, to call at a Coast Guard Marine Inspect:
office and explain the change made on the original certificate of discharge
for service on the SS FLAGSTAFF VICTORY and file an affidavit covering the
loss of your original certificate of discharge from the SS CHALMETTE. You
should advise this office as to what Marine Inspection office you will call.

The following is a correct record of your service on these vessels in
accordance with our files:

SS WAR BONNET	Second Cook	9-13-46 to	10-15-46
SS FLAGSTAFF VICTORY	Assistant Cook	11-8-46 to	1-13-47
SS CHALMETTE	Utilityman	2-1-47 to	3-6-47
SS LA BREA HILLS	Wiper	3-24-49 to	6-3-49

Very truly yours,

R. H. FARINHOLT
Commander, USCG
Chief, Merchant Vessel Personnel
Records and Welfare Section

93

REFERENCES OF DAD'S SHIP

What Dad went through can be seen in the second document.   **S.S LUCRECIA**.

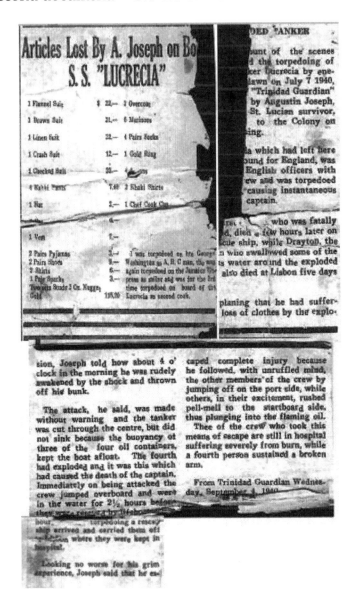

THIS WAS THE "S.S.LUCRECIA DOCUMENT

We are all very proud of these, it's certainly helped me understand as an adult why I found Dad's behaviour wanting as a child.

THIS WAS DAD'S CERTIFICATE
OF DISCHARGE DATED 1960

CHAPTER FOUR

I REALLY DO NOT LIKE THIS HOUSE

I think it was 1971 when we moved to a new house, the season had to be Winter because we were not in there long before the decimal currency was announced. My sister Sheila's 10th birthday was on that same day February 15th. Boy did she lap it up, "nobody is ever going to forget my birthday now, it's famous."

She was right, I never forgot the date.

This house was completely different, tiny in comparison to St Peter's Road, and long. It was a terrace so you could hear the plumbing from Mr Shadier next door. 111 Stamford Road it was, Oh my life! I really did not like that house.

It had a side sloping alley to the back gate that revealed a long garden, but the garden had nothing in it. Nothing at all except two silly little, could have been small conifers plonked in the middle of a lawn, one on each side of a path. My thoughts on this garden? Dead! There would be no Treehouse and where would the chickens go? Dad would have the time of his life with a completely blank canvas. He would have to build a shed, the coup, and a greenhouse, something for him to get stuck into.

As for school, well that, would be a long way away now, was I expected to walk with Pam all that way? This made me feel out of my depth, being out of control was the thing I didn't relish.

Now I was really drowning.

The house for its sins, did at least have two living rooms and Uncle would not be having any of them not this time. Thank you, God. One was for best which pleased Mother, so both Mom and Dad had something they could showcase.

I can see it now the finished article, our highly polished mahogany and walnut furniture, with the radiogram taking pride of place, each ornament strategically placed on top of a decorative lace doily starched stiff for maximum effect. Crochet mats of varied sizes to mount the glass cabinet, the bar, the gram, and the backs of the chairs and sofa.

Beyond these two rooms came a galley-type kitchen. I could see Dad was not impressed but it did at least have an adjacent lean-to larder with a clear roof, nice and bright in there. It was perfect for our blue larder unit, everyone had one of those back then.

Following on from the kitchen came the bathroom and then a separate toilet. I immediately thought "*oh dear,* night time wee, there must be another one upstairs."

The hallway, sorry the space between the front door and the stairs, I mean it was so narrow I could almost touch both walls. It was only enough space to cater for the two living room doorways with a few spare feet to the front door. It became the telephone area in later years and our acrobatic corridor to play 'L' Ups (Lift ups) in.

Mom was quick to cover the carpet with a long piece of plastic to prevent dirt entering the rest of the house, but it was nothing like she was used to. Now how was she going to keep this tiny poor excuse of a house clean with us lot running around it and getting under her feet?!

There were three bedrooms upstairs, Desmond had one all to himself as usual. It was the first door you saw as the stairs ended; I bet now he was glad he was the only boy. Mom and Dad would have the biggest which was to the front of the house, you could see the road from the window with a row of houses and windows staring straight back at you, *lovely.*

The other bedroom at the back of the house, was to hold all six of us. I'm not kidding you, we had the same beds but in our old house it was only two in each. Now as we could only fit two double beds in the room, three of us would be in each bed. So then the war commenced. We fought like 'Tom and Jerry,' remember. This top and tailing was nothing we weren't already used to but now there were six of us and in a smaller room, this caused added friction.

I was at the bottom of one bed, and Pam the bottom of the other. It was worse than just the squashing up factor, there was no upstairs loo after all. The loo was now just the potty in our room. I wasn't long in potty training to start with. Now I had to succumb to the humiliation of sharing a piss pot with my five sisters in a small room, *what the hell!*

All that you can imagine, did happen, doing our business when the pot was brimming, the splashback. Well it was either that or take the long walk downstairs to the very end of the house to use the loo. No, I really did not like that house at all.

So that was it there was nothing more to see so we sat amongst the bags and boxes, and then Mother poured us a glass of milk. Mom and Dad looked at each other. I never witnessed that look before, and it made me feel sad because they looked sad.

The van pulled up outside and chaos ensued,

"come out from under mi foot, gwarn in a de garden."

When Mother broke out in patois she meant business. We retreated to the 'very exciting garden'. I'm being sarcastic of course.

Martha had an idea, "let's take the line down and play skipping."

I saw this at school, but I wasn't asked to join in with anyone not that I got the chance being lumbered with Pam all the time.

Martha tied one end to the fence post and started to swing the other end round and round. She then sang this song about your birthday,

"when it's your birthday, please jump in, January, February, March, April, May, June," and so it went on.

I couldn't believe it last; I was last even in a game of bloody skipping, I was last.

Martha was born in January, but she was turning the rope, so she didn't count. Sheila in February, Jenna in April, Sarah in May, even Pam was August, me being September meant I jumped last and by then everyone's legs were tired and they messed up the jump, so I only got to do a few leaps.

It seemed like ages outside and it was getting cold. We raced up and down for a bit, jumping over the little conifers on the lawn.

It gave Jenna another idea, "let's play leapfrog" she said.

"Well you're not jumping over my back you're too fat," said Sheila.

She still hasn't much tact or diplomacy to this day and I don't suppose it's her fault. She would have been quite special for a bit being the new sister to Martha then we all came after. What a blow for her. I came to my sister's defense not even sure why; all I knew was that I felt like I did on the playground when the others were making remarks about Pam.

"If I jump over you Chookley, you can jump over me."

"Okay, Bebby would get it wrong anyway," she claimed.

Of course, I still let Pam have a try after all, I wanted her off my back.
If she got this right at home she could try it at school couldn't she! And then she would leave me alone. The garden with its two lanes of grass either side of the path was good for races, so we had two teams. Me and Chookley versus Sheila and Martha. Sarah was always coughing and sometimes her legs played up, so she sat out. Pam tried for a bit but found it difficult to get over our backs, so she watched.

We played for a considerable length of time and we actually had fun not one bit of squabbling, just laughing as we repeatedly fell.

The leapfrog lead to wheelbarrows and various types of the same such as piggybacking.

On the path, Sarah drew out some squares in white and put numbers on them.

"What's that you're drawing sis?" Jenna and I said at the same time.

"Arr, you're in trouble that's chalk you got that from school!" Said Jenna.

"It was on the floor anyway and it's not just me that does it we play this on the playground so there."

Sarah protested assertively then continued with her own game of 'hopscotch'.

Soon we were all joining in. I'd never noticed this game before, she learned it from school of course.

She was very happy to show off about it especially as we didn't deem her fit enough to join in with the running or leapfrog to begin with. It wasn't long before she was running and jumping over those conifers herself and faster than us too sometimes. Sarah is a real trier; she always was and still is. I admire that in her I really do.

"I'm missing out," I thought, being with Pam was proving educationally costly. Everything was finally done well as much as it could be. All the boxes and bags would take more time to get through.

"Come inside now and wash your hands," Mom shouted from the window.

Dad had cooked seasoned rice. Seasoned rice was rice of course with cabbage, onions and pieces of sausage and bacon. As there was very little meat the rice and cabbage filled it out. Clever Dad lots of mouths to feed; he was used to that from the Navy days.

It was a Saturday, we usually have soup but that would have taken too long, a good thing as by now it was very late no time really to do his famous throw it all in soup. In twos we had a bath nothing different there. Only as there was one bathroom with one tank of water, Pam and I had to use the same water as Chookley and Sarah, so it got a bit cold.

Mother must have been very busy upstairs sorting out the furniture and making the beds.

Sorry Mom but it wasn't as good as when Mrs. Campbell did them. The beds were very close together not much room to get around because the wardrobe and chest of drawers had to also have a place.

It wasn't a good first night's sleep, I was thinking about wanting a wee plus Jenna's foot kept resting on me. Sarah snored because of her bronchitis; it was a very long night indeed. Besides the snoring and the plumbing from next door I could hear something else, something I couldn't describe. A scratching and scurrying in the wall cavities. .

Sunday morning Mom and Dad were up early, sorting stuff out. Dad had several mouse traps in his hands and blue poison.

"Don't touch any of these," he said with authority after he positioned them in the corners.

I didn't yet know what a mouse looked like, but I soon would. Mother went out shortly after we were up washed and dressed so we were left with Dad. Gosh, we were all bored. There was nothing on the television worth watching either no, I really did not like that house.

Due to us going to a Church of England school when Mother come back she told us that as of the following week we were to attend church. We all thought it was the school church but no it wasn't, this church would last all day serves our rights for complaining of boredom.

School was now the most attractive thought and I couldn't wait for Monday, Pam or no Pam.

That evening after dinner, we all sat to watch 'Songs of Praise.' You won't believe the audacity of those mice, warriors they were, scurrying about right in front of us like they owned the place. Well, maybe they did have it to themselves before we moved in, but it was our house now, so they had better just move out. You would have laughed if you had seen the synchronised movement of our feet; leaping up to be cradled with our arms on the sofa, in a two-handed swoop.

All together, we yelped "ahh! What was that!" Dad knew, mom knew, now we all knew what mice were.

"It's alright, let them gwarn, dem soon dead." Dad said in a convincing form of patois, and he was right.

The next morning, three were strangled by the traps. Unfortunately during the night, Martha, on the very long journey to the loo, stepped barefooted straight onto a mouse corpse. It must have been poisoned and tried to get back into the walls. It went through her toes, she was quick to divulge to us in the most descriptive manner, "it squelched and oozed covering the top of my foot;" she said.

No way was I ever going to the loo in the night. I'm not having any mice on me; I will use that potty even if it was brimming.

The following Sunday night, boy, did I want to. Mom always insisted on us all having a weekly wash out, or bowel cleanse. The laxatives of choice were either a kind of chocolate called 'Brooklax,' or the very bitter Senna leaves carefully boiled, strained, and cooled. Pam didn't like to drink the senna water, neither did we, but only she could get away without having it.

She was always given the chocolate alternative, and we would only have that if the Senna ran out. Mother was very clever with the dose. It was always just the right amount, which gave you a comfortable release, ready to take another week of school dinners, because school dinners we're so starchy and dense.

On one particular occasion, I already had my dose of Senna, so why I thought I was deprived of the chocolate one and insisted I had some of Pam's by snatching a chunk from her hand, was beyond me. Serves me right, my stomach twisted and knotted, cut me up good and proper. It felt like my stomach was doing a breaststroke, trying to make its way through my intestines, to escape via my arse, I was growling so much.

The potty was full, but I needed it, and I needed it badly. I squatted and tried to allow a small amount out just enough to ease the crippling pain I was now experiencing, oh no! It wasn't going to comply with that.

Who was I kidding, trying to squeeze and hold like an icing bag. I looked around desperately for something, anything for it to go in. Gosh, I can't believe I'm divulging this, anyway, shit happens, right?!

I filled my school shoes, both of them, but it still wasn't containable. I was leaking like a drainpipe in a storm. Sarah's shoes, I could see them, I had no damned choice, believe me, I had to let the full force of what was left go. I blew like a fog horn, how the hell nobody woke up is beyond me. What a beautiful sense of relief!

Sweating and shaking, it was that intense. I covered the two pairs of shoes with my pillowcase, the smell was too much still, so I put my pillow over them too. *'I must get up early and clean them; I'm dead if I don't.'*

I lay back in bed for a short while but couldn't sleep. No, I'd done it now! The journey to the loo was more frightening than taking a dump in our shoes, I can tell you. But getting caught after doing such a thing, *I'll be as dead as that mouse that Martha unfortunately squashed.* I had to face the mice; it was me against them.

Mrs. Campbell and Yvette entered my head; they would smash them. I think I was beginning to miss those two. I managed to get there and did my best.

I really did clean out the shoes, but I was afraid to put on the light. The light meant a mouse would jump on me. They were warriors, and I was on their turf. It was their territory, and they were in the walls, what if one leaped out and bit my face?

I poured the poo into the loo then scooped out the rest with my hand. Oh my god, it went all over the seat I was making things worse by the second.

Eventually, I did a fair, clean up and used lots of Dettol to clean out the shoes, wash off the seat and clean my hands, was it good enough? Hell no! To think Dad only polished them on Friday ready for school.

The morning came, and immediately, everyone said, "who shit up the place" because of the spots on the carpet, I was leaking like a drainpipe.

Of course, I never said a word, but as soon as Sarah saw my face and her shoes…

No time to procrastinate, we had to get ready and quick, being late for school meant, 'Mr. Stanly.'

Thank goodness, I now knew how to comb hair. I found I was to do both my own and Pam's all the time. Two bunches was all I could manage that day, but at least it was neat. Sarah and I ended up wearing our Plimsolls, she didn't speak to me for a week. Giving me sucked teeth and slitty side eyes.

The walk was onerous, up Stamford road, along Putney, over Roberts and Hunters, then up Church-Lane, dragging Pam.

This was so unfair to me; the others just up and went, not giving us a second thought. In a way, I suppose it was a saving grace; we were never early enough to have any morning playtime, so no teasing.

As we entered the gates, the bell went, Phew! Can't keep this up I thought! Something is going to give I'm sure of it. Inside, straight to the assembly we go, "All things bright and beautiful" Mrs. Rudder at the piano, with her little frame and soft hands. Mrs. Hackett front and centre, she was the head. Far right, Mr. Stanly, half singing and half peering out the window to see who would dare try to sneak in late.

I quite enjoyed assembly, I liked singing. Sometimes, some of the older pupils would play the recorder and bang the tambourine.?

When will I get to do that? I thought. With me being taken from class to sit with Pam at least twice if not three times out of the five days, chances were slim.

It was a difficult time for me, worst for Pam, I'm sure, the whole damned term went before Pam settled, and I was never to be called to the medical room again.

Finally, I begin to grow, more importantly, so did Pam. Her talking at home about school was great. The more she had to talk about, the more it helped her practice her speech and slowed down her stuttering episodes.

I began to get plenty of music time with Mrs. Rudder, loved it, a wonderful new escapism.

I think, with us all beginning to develop our individual personalities, the quarreling and wanting space, in our now small house, the usual pushing and odd slap, became much, much worse.

Fine, there's nothing wrong with a bit of sibling rivalry except with it came barbaric beatings. Our new chosen pastimes in school became so very important, we all now needed much encouragement and friendships to sustain us.

Spare the Rod Spoil the Child

Sundays, we began with church followed by Sunday school. It started at 11 am and ended at 4 pm, and we hated it. A big blue van would come and collect us, and we would suffer the five long hours.

The singing and clapping were great, really happy; it was the Bible bit that freaked us out. It wasn't like the school church; it was scary.

People jumping and shouting next to you and falling on the floor, kicking, throwing their arms about, I thought some of them were swearing. I'm older now, of course, and also a 'Believer.' They were simply caught up in giving their praises unto the Lord. The perceptions ignorance can give, eh!

We weren't keen on church after that and tried umpteen amount of excuses to get out of going, but all to no avail. We were going, come what it may.

I'm so grateful to Mother's persistence on that issue. Getting closer to God throughout my life has prevented and protected me in so many ways, from things I may not have been able to divert from.

God works in mysterious ways. "Suffer the little children to come unto me" and come we did eventually.

Now, God is firmly placed at the centre of all our lives.

We were all getting older; the look we used to get off Mom the one that stopped us in our tracks, didn't wash as well, it just failed to have the same effect. We fought for our space, we fought for our share, I was used to doing that already, but now the others had to do that too.

Somehow, I was now quietly ahead emotionally. It's not that I was ever first, second, even third, for anything, so as I watched them become more and more perplexed, that feeling of power within me, increased. That house had miraculously changed the equilibrium. From the days of tapping my feet on my sister Pam's chest to pacify her in the pram, to now, I had been hard done by.

Seeing how my sisters' faces changed with uncertainties about life, when I felt quite calm was empowering. This new weakness of theirs, however, wasn't nice to witness. Whether it was because we were in different schools or simply hormonal, the separations and the secretiveness, cost them the strap.

Being stuck in the same room as we grew, wasn't comfortable for any of us, and those frustrations made us less accommodating to each other. We became lazy and selfish., it wasn't so easy to just pass the buck, as we were all sticking up for ourselves by then.

We would get the buckle end of the belt, the broom handle, the slipper, the switch, 'a long branch with lots of giving' much like the school cane and the curtain wire.

Anything at hand really and when we were struck, father would administer each blow with every syllable to a word.

"If, you, think, you, can, just, help, yourself, do, what, you, want?!" Hmm!

The navy, his home upbringing, the move, I don't know, but I've never seen such wickedness. We fought like cat and mouse, yes, but now we would do our best to contain it and not let Mom or Dad see. We were scared to death!

We were bonding differently, comforting each other after a thorough beating, Jenna seemed to be a regular target.

One day, all she did God bless her was help herself to Dad's favourite biscuits, 'Ritz Crackers'. When he came in from God knows where as usual, straight to the larder he'd go, he liked to have a cup of tea with them before cooking dinner for us.

None of us were ever foolish enough to eat unless we were given something, snacking just wasn't done, Mom and Dad knew what we had in the house, Dad more than Mom as he did more of the cooking.

I remember us all awaiting Dad to serve us up our dinner, but he was in the garden we had at least another hour and half.

We decided to play a game to fill the time. 'I spy with my little eye something beginning with....' 'leg' said Sheila to Martha, 'you always say something to do with the sideboard, before even giving Martha a chance she suggests we play 'L' Ups instead which is our lifting up each other game, I see Jenna's face drop. No filter has Sheila. We play okay for a bit 'get up straight Jannette see if you can touch the ceiling'

I try to stretch up on Sheila's shoulders to reach but even together We're still too short. Where's Jenna, we all look for Jenna realising that she's not joined in, we find Jenna balancing by the cupboard on the kitchen stool.

Daddy's Ritz

Daddies favourite biscuits were 'Ritz' if you touched that red box expect to get 'licks'.

Don't try to be clever don't try to be smart, by taking out only a few; he's counted them already 'cacafart' My poor sister Choockley took it upon herself to put the stool next to the cupboard shelf, she then took down that red box of Ritz, she never ate just some she finished the whole box of it, well near enough as only a bit was left.

So, she put the box back into its exact same space and sat with us on the settee with crumbs on her face.
We all looked at Jenna and shook our heads, Jenna, said "Martha, if Daddy finds out you know you're dead."

Daddy came in and made himself a cup of tea, pulled down his red box of Ritz to find it was empty. We interlock arms and start to rock on the settee.

"A who tek mi Ritz talk up which one a you?"

"Not me Daddy, I would never do that to you."

Martha spoke first then Sheila, Sarah and me so Daddy took off his belt to Choockley. Six of the best wailed up her back and leg, "mi nar do it agen Daddy" a so she a beg.

"You can't hear so you must feel" every time Daddy hit her, we all rock and squeal.

Daddy's beatings always brought out our sistership, the caring nature of us all. It wasn't long before Sheila came along changing the scene to her tending to Jenna with the all-important tub of white petroleum Vaseline.

We all sat on the sofa in a row, rocking like robots after witnessing that, Sheila tried, as usual, to administer the petroleum jelly to every wail; she was very kind mannered when you were in need. If someone had pictured that they would have said; "that's the image of children with mental health issues." Every one of us today still rock, thank God we haven't suffered with our mental health to the point of sectioned treatment.

Beatings of this severity became our normal way of life, everyone in those days got a beating and at school too. It got to the point you would compare your parents' strategies with your peers and show your bruising or wails.

Different times now, the teacher can't even comfort a child who has fallen on the playground or take pictures of the school play. Boundaries and barriers, some for the better, others have proven for the worst.

I got 'the hand' off Mr. Stanly once myself, and 'the ruler' was not going to be enough after what I said and did. He pulled me by my ear, using it as a tow rope to the rest of my body; it really hurt. He raised my skirt to reveal my navy-blue tights, and then six big slaps.

Do you know, I never flinched one bit; the ear pulling was far worse. Mr. Stanly though, he was sweating, tough as boots, by then, I was more confident and more assertive.

I knew after that, Uncle Clinton would never lick his finger and draw over my vagina, pull his bulging zip and try to entice me with pear drops or anything else.

Now I was stronger and a beating was just a beating. I could, I felt, stand up to it all, and the school became my fortress; I was the ruler of my space. We all found that school was proving to be a valuable asset in our lives. Home life had many drawbacks, with the overcrowding, the extra squabbles, unbelievable beatings and our own individual growth.

Mrs. Campbell and Yvette, a distant memory, I longed to see them. The chores we now had to contemplate were so tasking. You don't know what you've got until it's taken away, that's for sure a lesson I'll take to the grave. Come back Mrs. Campbell; all is forgiven.

Sweeping was the hardest for me; the broom handle was too long, and I didn't mind washing the clothes over the bath. I enjoyed getting the block of carbolic soap and mimicking Mrs. Campbell. The wringing out, however, split my hands between the thumb and forefinger, thank goodness for good old-fashioned petroleum jelly.

I believe, today, that it would have been considered, 'workhouse conditions'. One winter, I thought I was doing a good thing; I put the clothes out on the line. It wasn't too bad, nice, and windy, it turned to frost though.

When Mother came back from work she said, "who put the clothes them outside?"

I quickly said, "it was me," waiting for some praise. Am I finally going to be seen, am I finally going to be acknowledged for doing good?

"Well, you better call de clothes dem to cum, dem so damn stiff dem can walk in dem owna self."

Patois! Oh no, I was in trouble. Sure enough, I got a backhander across my head, but it wasn't too bad, more of a… you stupid girl kind of hit. The hurt of not being praised for trying to do a good thing was more painful.

We may have consoled one another after a beating, but that was certainly counterbalanced by the, 'every man for himself, get out of that chore syndrome'. Tom and Jerry, more like fox and hound, we tore ribbons off one another, pushing, scratching, even biting, we were feral.

I'm totally and utterly embarrassed by that revelation, but it was true, dog eats dog.

The school was our only individual time, the only wonderful attention we got, and friends. We were having outside relationships that hadn't a clue about the goings on behind 111 Stamford Road doors, a completely unbiased opinion of who we were and how we could actually be. These new emotions were truly great, medicinal, almost, and I became an addict to its influence.

Saturday had the most chores, and Sunday was church almost all day long. Monday couldn't come soon enough, even with the ugliest oldest clothes, I didn't even care if I got the ruler or six slaps. I knew I only fought in my sister's defense, so it made me feel honorable.

The school was still the best thing since sliced bread, my new Treehouse. Speaking of bread, we got very routine in that new house. Monday was wash day, and the meal was whatever Dad could do with the Sunday's leftovers.

All the washing had to be dried indoors; during winter, we would still have to fetch the paraffin from the corner shop, then fill the heaters, which smelt bad. Mind you, even the pretty patterns of light it made on the ceiling couldn't compensate, that smell was toxic.

Nobody wanted to go down the road to the corner shop to fetch the paraffin because it was heavy to carry. I was only six years old, but I still had to take my turn to fetch it.

"I'm not going again, I went last week Monday, and it's raining," said Martha and "Sarah can't go not in this weather, you have to go Jannette, Sarah will have to take your turn next week if it's not raining just put Mommy's rain hat on."

If it wasn't your turn you didn't have to go, that was one job I wasn't pushed into that and laundry day where taken in turns equally.

It never made a difference what age we were or that we were almost, all girls, the chores needed doing, heavy difficult or dangerous it just had to be done.

Tuesday was mainly polishing of the silver and cleaning the glassware. Another light meal of corned beef or sardines and rice. Wednesday, Dad puts on the television found a western film, put up the ironing board as per usual and did the mountain of ironing. That day, it was tripe or cow's feet with butter beans and spuds from the garden. Thursday, we did outside, yes, we cleaned the bins inside and out, swept the front yard and the back path down before washing the windows with Windolene and paper. I almost drank it once because it looked like the blancmange from school; good thing I smelt it first.

Can you imagine getting kids of today to do all that?! Wrapped in cotton wool now, they are and not always for the greater good either.

How things have changed, they don't know how to do anything practical; give them something technical though, they blow you away.

Having their own lunch money, not a great idea. They're not being sensible enough to buy what's good for them. We, on the other hand, all had school dinners; it's a good thing too, okay. They were tasteless, but the puddings made up for it. Chocolate concrete, Spotted dick, Chocolate crispies, and the Blancmange of course.

There is no way on earth Mom and Dad could afford to give all of us dinner money; routine chores, routine dinners at school and at home, the structure I suppose provided consistency.

When I think of the amount of chemicals we were exposed to, without a hint of instruction, criminal, did we come to any harm!? I think we had more common sense because we were left to our own devices, talk about finding things out the hard way.

Friday, of course, was fish and chips from the local chippy, with lemonade, awesome treat. Only a small chore that day; shoe polishing with 'Cherry blossom', Dad did that anyway and got out every scuff that stuff, brilliant. We didn't have a bag of fish and chips each that would have been far too expensive, so three portions were bought, and we shared them out. A little bit of paper eating, and sucking was done too as it was so delicious.

"Can I have the paper to chew this time Jenna, I think you had the last one,"

"erm, no you can't not all of it only half,"

"mmm tar."

Jenna, Pam and I shared because Pam didn't eat much, Martha, Sheila and Sarah shared because Sarah didn't eat much, the other portion was between Mom, Dad and Desmond.

Saturday was soup with everything and anything in it, best being the dumplings. For chores, all the inside doors, frames, etc., sorting of clothes and repairs.

Sunday, a full roast after church, so no chores. Then back to Monday, same, same, same. We were eager for change, that's when we noticed our neighbours, but, were not yet prepared to make friends with them, just observe for now.

Across the road, there was a black and an Asian family; the Asians had a different clothes sense than ours. We never saw them at school, so they must be at a different school we thought. I suppose if they went to St Mary's like us, we would have been friends straight away.

Up the road, only a few doors up, another black family, they were bigger and scary, no, we didn't intend to make friends with them anytime soon; we would avoid them if we could. We would watch them play on the road regularly, but they also had Stamford Grove, so you would see them running in and out from it. It made us curious, but not enough to ask to play with them, not for a year or so anyway.

We played together as siblings and became masters of new games, we climbed down the stairs in various ways; did handstands, cartwheels, and balancing on each other's shoulders along the tiny corridor space between the stairs and front door. We were bonding.

Yes, we fought like cat and dog, but when we bonded, it was as cement. We were all very inventive, and the imaginative streak passed through us all.

I have from time to time wondered what each of my siblings, 'Treehouse' was, their escape? Or indeed if they needed one?

When I look back, I think my sister Sarah had the best childhood, weird really as she was always sickly. So much attention she got though, would you Adam and Eve it, she's only a nurturing motivational speaker now, with her own company. She does all that yoga and holistic teaching along with beauty techniques.

Yes, indeed, she certainly is giving what she got, and she never had a beating or any abuse either. I rest my case.

CHAPTER FIVE

SHEILA MARIA'S SCHOOL OF DANCE

As we each developed through schooling also came the after-school accolades, sports club. I was good at running, rounders, and netball. Not surprising, as pulling Pam to school was leg strengthening alright.

I was chosen for the athletic team, one hundred metres, eight hundred, fifteen hundred, and relay team. It wasn't easy being in the teams; there was practice to consider. This is where my sisters outdid themselves in their response towards me, especially as I thought we were beginning to bond. I asked them all to help take it in turns to look after Pam, so I could go to practice, and they all said, "no."

I already had no choice in pulling Pam to school every weekday and taking her home. Now, I had sports practice straight after.

You would think sickly Sarah would volunteer, perhaps Jenna, not a chance. I had to run, dragging Pam crying behind me back home with the whole world looking, thinking I'm a cruel sister, then run back to school. Everyone else by then was well into their practice when I come darting in like a freight train.

"Where have you been?" The P.E. teacher would stress,

"sorry miss, but I have to take Pam home first."

"Is this to be a regular occurrence?"

"I think so miss, but it's running miss, so I'm practicing."

The others all laughed, so I exaggerated the comment by running on the spot then doing star jumps just to show I wasn't bothered but I so was. I could sense the teacher thought this to be unfair also.

"Okay, I'll make allowances."

I hated the look the others gave me for that response. Pam made me very fast, and able to sustain the longer distances. Already, she was making me better, I said so, didn't I? A lot of who I am stems back to Pam.

I put all my anger and frustrations into the sport; I was good at it too. This newfound empowering was very important, the pendulum always swinging from 'poor hard done by me,' subject to freezing at the point I should stamp my feet, to handling a damned good beating and running paces ahead of my peers.

God kept giving me something to rise above, something to learn from and develop; I'm so in awe of Him now.

During this period, my sister Sheila came across a dance school; I don't know if the others were interested, but I think it charged too.

I was always up for a challenge, anything new, but Mother didn't want Sheila to go alone. In fact, she always told us to go anywhere in twos, perhaps come to think, our only solid advice. In hindsight, she said this, when we came to the new house,

"when you go to your uncle, make sure it's two of you, or more."

Hmm! She flipping knew alright, can't ask the dead, though, can you? Gosh, Mother, WHY? Thank you for allowing me to go dancing school, but somehow, I feel it was a guilty payoff.

The dancing school was called, Sheila Maria's. You had the beginner's class, the intermediate, and the advanced. There were different age groups, and we found ourselves in the beginners. We knew nothing yet; Sheila got the correct age group.

I, unfortunately, looked too small and too young for my age, so they put me with the two to five-year-olds, I was mortified, I was nearly seven by then. We did nothing but tumbling, the odd cartwheel here and there and a very small amount of tap.

This went on for a period of six months, then the breakthrough, we were about to partake in our first performance. Rehearsals started, and they were intense. We had to get on the number eleven bus to go to the dancing school; this was going to prove tasking because, yes, you guessed it, I would have to take Pam home from school first.

Sometimes, Sheila just went off without me. I'm seven now and having to run to the bus stop on my own in the darkness of the Autumn and Winter months. Sheila, as per usual, didn't give me a second thought. It's a wonder I'm still alive; thank you, God.

We were supposed to get there on time for warm-ups you see, not only that, Sheila was out to be noticed, her extraordinary trait from very early on, I guess I may have also been the same. I was warm when I arrived alright, lying to them, that I had just been dropped off. They knew we had a car because we were taken in the car, to begin with.

As with school, Mom and Dad would be in trouble if they knew I'd come on the bus by myself. Not that Sheila was bothered, as long as she got there on time, everything was just fine and dandy.

The pressure was on, and she wanted to be picked for a good part in the show; lateness wouldn't be seen favourably. We had a deadline, hence the intensity. The lowest ages showcase was about a teddy bear, and I grew to hate the song. These are the words: *me and my teddy bear, we've got no worries, and we've got no cares, 'cause me and my teddy bear, we play and play all day.*

Sheila had a lovely ballet showcase with gymnastic pieces, and she got her way. I wanted and knew I could do her part; she knew it too, because I actually helped her practice at home. Any chance we got we would practice, Sheila asked me to hold her legs up against the wardrobe like a split, so she could stretch.

"Hold my leg up then come on, higher than that,"

"I can't I'm too short,"

"well come around then and push me from the back, gosh Jannette use your damn back,"

"I'm trying Sheila."

After stretches she would get me to be the markers of where she needed to be on the stage and clap her in we could only do it in the small space in the hallway hardly ideal I actually enjoyed it as it made me feel like a teacher, but then she teased me brutally about having to endure the juvenile showcase.

The family all came to see the show, and Mother and Father were finally going to see me. For the first time ever, it was going to be about me.

When the show ended, on the way home, Mother began singing the teddy bear song. I wanted to cry, she was proud of me, but somehow, my cocky alter ego reared its head, and I became smug instead. The song was repeated every day and anytime I entered a room at home, the attention I craved, I now regretted terribly.

Serves me right again, I thought, be careful what you wish for. In my own young way, there was no pleasing me.

All that time waiting to be numero uno, then complaining about it when it finally came, seven though, with a teddy bear song hanging over me. I didn't even like 'watch with Mother' at three years old. Juvenile, all of it, every time I think I'm getting somewhere, beginning to know who I am, the carpet, not just a rug, is pulled.

I wanted to be noticed and loved for what I did but now I felt too old for it, would anything in my life ever feel fair and just right?

There it was, I didn't even realise how blessed I'd been, no perception. I know I was young, but it was as if I had only two emotions; anger frustration if you like and happiness, where was my in between?

I learned plenty from Sheila Maria's, character-building being one of them; we were taught how to perform, and I used a lot of that teaching to talk to myself. I didn't realise I was learning more about my characters. My alter ego grew when I was chosen for parts in the school plays, it didn't need to be amplified. It kind of gave me a sense of loss, because I was praised for being someone or something else on stage when I really wanted to be praised for just being me. I couldn't always face me, not in full, not in my entirety.

The real me was introvert, if I hadn't got something or someone to control or mask my emotions, I simply felt out of my depth.

Who the hell was I? First, I'm given the nickname 'Batman'. That's not real. I don't know why I was given that name. I only made up my own theory, thinking Mom and Dad thought me a fighter for good, not just because I became unruly. I knew Batman was two people, even at that age.

I'm put in charge of my sister before I could even fully wash and dress myself. I mean, who does that? No wonder I didn't find children's television particularly stimulating. I was never allowed to be childlike, was I? I truly hadn't a clue who I was.

I'm still putting a character to every scenario I face. Yes, I was happy I suppose that I was good at things, lots of things, but was I just mimicking and hiding?

Getting friends wasn't easy, I was avoided, perhaps it was my arrogance. I wanted to be noticed for the right reasons, I always pined for that, but I tried too hard, I think. So instead of appearing friendly, I came across unnaturally scary and a bit bossy. I could feel the tension when I couldn't see the faces, I'll tell you the truth, it's still happening to me now.

I'm Going to Have to Work Even Harder

It took me a longtime to realise I was doing things for the wrong reasons. It wasn't the way to love and respect myself. I wanted to be seen, yes, but I had to learn how to do things not just for my benefit. Whether it was seen or not wasn't the point; attention wasn't the do all and end all.
Not having the chance to be just me, had fogged my perception so much. I didn't know how to, not act out and show people what I thought they wanted to see; school was the chance to bring me out. Pam was in every year, though and at the back of my mind constantly. I didn't know how to detach from her, yet, I was so desperate to.

I may have had the after-school clubs, but she still came first. How was I ever going to just be me, without the alter ego, if Pam was always there? *'I'm going to have to work even harder,'* I thought. When I did, however, again, it wasn't really me, I just didn't cope very well. My frustration with myself and not being able to differentiate between my true self and my alter ego, utter disappointment over Uncle, all culminated into self-harming instead. I'm not yet nine years old.

The seventies was the era of power cuts, so we always had candles. I found a strange sense of relief when I accidentally got burned with some hot wax; it was a new feeling for a start. At every opportunity, I regularly took the candle and made the hot wax drip over my inner thighs. It was an area that caused trouble for me with Uncle anyway, maybe I thought I could remember that feeling instead of the frozen locked in syndrome he gave me. All I know is, the initial surge of instant pain just helped release everything else, and the inner me came to the surface.

There were many power cuts, so plenty of opportunities to carry out my ritual. Once I had that, I found I needed other harsh encounters to bring me a similar false sense of relief. A popular game called 'hot ball' started at school, and you had to run in various directions to avoid the sting of the ball that was thrown at full speed and intensity, purposefully to hit you; this was my replacement of wax. I could hardly bring the candle to school and light it; me, and a box of Swan Vestas! I'd be expelled in an instant. It was an okay substitute if I made sure I got hit as often as I could.

"You're spoiling the game you are,"

"yeah who still wants Jannette to play?"

"Not me,"

"nor me Jannette keeps running across on purpose in front of the ball stopping the game."

"Yeah silly! You're supposed to run away from it, if you don't play it properly, we're not playing with ya."

Everything became a battle of wills, my true self against my alter ego. I always started off as me, and then it would creep in; I even talked differently. If only I could have been allowed to be a child and grow up at a natural pace! *I must work even harder.*

Finally, I found something calming, reading. The Peter and Jane books, they were about relationships within the family, friends, and pets.

These gave me an insight as to how the other pupils at school lives, maybe, so I started to observe their playing, listen to their laughter, and imagine their home lives. I could feel my alter ego inflame me, a sense of jealousy, and there it was, that's how I had to separate. I'm a kid, how do I start to learn how?

The true me enjoyed watching the others, and my other side felt envy and hurt. *I never had any of that; it's not fair, it's all their fault, it's Uncle's fault, it's Pam's fault, blame, blame, blame.*

I found I could now tell myself to shut up and could work at getting the better side to be more dominant, even though it was shy.

All that time of being in control, wasn't, the true me, but I didn't like the feeling of not being in control at all. It was a suppressed feeling, was it because I didn't have a chance to grow?

I questioned myself daily, and every time I felt nervous and out of my depth, I worked harder at how I felt rather than dismissing it and letting old bossy boots step in. I breathed it out, calmed myself and accepted the emotions. Wow! It was okay; not great, but okay.

I started to attract friends with my now softer approach, kinder voice, and no more brutal fighting. Daddy made me want to hit the bullies at school because they teased Pam, I really had to try hard not to fight. When I did something wrong to Pam or made her do something, she shouldn't I was punished.

It's funny how I soon was able to spot the new bullies because they got braver, thinking I'd softened; no longer was I the talk of the playground, or kept away from. Pam attracted her own friends too, much to my delight, she really could be very funny indeed if given the chance to. They stayed away from her because they didn't want the wrath of Jan, that's what everyone called me for short. "Everyone ran from Jan!" An overture sang in the corners of the playground when they felt brave enough.

My new self-examination was proving invaluable. I had learned the art of reason; the true me was a real carer underneath, there! Mom and Dad were right after all; I was indeed the correct family member to have Pam as my ward. With maturity and new realisations, I was beginning not to blame everything and everyone, but rather accept and adapt.

Over time, with new friends and an acceptance of my circumstances, I began to quite like myself. With this, of course, came confidence, did I need Miss bossy boots alter ego anymore?

Oh, yes, I did, but now, I had complete control. I could call her out anytime I pleased; she was now just a changeable character, one that was quite humourous as well as fearless. My self-harming went in the cupboard, but not away entirely.

Uncle was still a parasitic memory, Pear drops and all. He didn't visit as much; maybe we were getting too old. We, however, were all developing.

There was a difference; none of us smiled or laughed much when he came around anymore. Not just me, had they all cottoned on?

It didn't matter, he still came, and we still visited him when asked to go. I had to wait forty-five years to realise the extent of his abuse. We all kept our own dirty little secret because we were programmed to.

The extent of the shame is the length and breadth of a lifetime because we will never have justice, and never have closure. The wages of sin is death, a Biblical verse in Romans; he's dead and gone, only God can judge him now.

CHAPTER SIX

THE NEIGHBOURS BECOME OUR GLUE

P eople bring out the best and worst in you; sometimes, you don't even realise how much a person's influences have rubbed off on you until someone else points them out. Without these varied influences, however, we would have no idea of our own strengths, depths, or capabilities. 'Variety is the spice of life' after all.

We all got brave and merged forward into the neighbourhood; all that initial resistance fading. To start with, we played our own games, and Desmond had made a go-kart, using our old pram, some timber and some rope for steering it.

That flipping pram I couldn't have been more delighted to see it broken to bits and turned into something I did want to go into. Once we had that on site, everyone wanted a go. If it wasn't the go-kart, it was Desmond's bike, it was a bright light green one with a white saddle he just grew out of it, what a hand me down! No complaints about that one. It was good of him to share it with us.

Our road was quite steep to one side, so you would go amazingly fast, great fun!

When we rode the bike in twos it was hilarious, "weeee! Ouch ohhh wait slow down ha ha ha my bottom ouch!" I said to Jenna.

"Wow! that was really good enit?"

Jenna was great on the bike doing standing riding, but that saddle was tough and the splits in the leather didn't help at all. Our relationship as siblings was a little fractious, but when we played…

The Asian and black families over the road; in fact, directly opposite, mended our broken wings and established a connection with us. They became our glue, which we knew was there, but were too busy trying to fight our own way into, or out of something, that it just became too awkward to really sustain a genuine closeness.

The Asians got beatings themselves; you could even hear theirs sometimes, coming out from the grove, so we knew they would understand us.

Oh, how we laughed when we compared our suffering, unbelievable isn't it? What a thing to compare, we did everything together.

That family had six children; three boys and three girls. Funny enough, I bonded with the second to last girl, and Sarah, the next one up, as we were in our own family. Not only were we the same in line, but near the same ages too! The black family, well, we only ever played with the girl Sharon, but she had a brother too. Our brother's age, so he wouldn't be playing with us.

They attended the school up the road, Westminster it was, no more than five hundred metres or so away. I couldn't believe it when they said they were sometimes late. We never saw them going to school in the mornings, of course, because they would have left after us. Due to the distance we had to go, we left at least a good half hour prior to them.

After our acquaintance developed somewhat, they were happy to tell us that they watched us going to school. I felt myself getting flushed, and they would soon mention me dragging Pam.

I held my breath.

"How come you guys go off and leave her, (me) to pull her (Pam) up the road?" asked Shazier.

Warmth and delight replaced the flush of embarrassment, I thought to myself, "they're on my side."

Sarah felt the pressure to answer, as Shazier was her new friend whom I'm sure she wanted to impress.

"Don't know, she's always done it, they're always together."

There it was in audio, they're always together she said just as I expected. I was invisible I was just expected then to be with Pam, wow! Somehow, I didn't feel a gloating sense of 'I knew it.'

Sarah didn't realise she was ignoring me so maybe the others didn't either, they didn't do it on purpose; they just did what they were always shown, what they were used to. It's true, I was always with Pam.

They were just themselves before she and I came along, and nothing changed for them. I came first, there was nothing abnormal about me, so things remained the same, then Pam came a year later, they couldn't have known anything was different about her for a while, so yes, they continued as before, nothing changed.

When it eventually did, all they saw was me with her all the time, because we were the last two and probably shared the same space so much that I was simply overlooked; then it was just as if we were one.

I got it now; they weren't to be blamed after all, none of them.

Immediately, I felt completely different towards my siblings and would start to do things I knew I was good at for them and help without making too much of a fuss. This was a new me, the real me, no longer would I have to wear my alter ego armour, I felt amazingly refreshed.

One afternoon when Mother was out, I found her Singer-sewing machine. I had seen her use it only once before, and that was very brief, but it was enough to whet my appetite. She was smooth with it, and I liked the noise it made as well as the action of the wheel and the concentration on Mother's face as she executed her mending.

I needed to know what to do with my clothes; elastic bands and safety pins were not good enough, they looked a better fit, but they still looked like they came out of a skip. The machine was the answer, and I had to learn. It was small and black, with the word Singer on the side in gold writing.

The wheel was stiff, but it was all set up with the thread in the bobbin. Being the inquisitive person, I am, I practiced how to use it, right there and then. Luckily, there were some pieces of fabric, all different types in a box underneath. This was my only chance, maybe, so I was going to grab it with both hands; if she caught me, what could I get that I hadn't got a thousand times. It was worth a good beating to have better clothes.

I practiced over and over until I was satisfied, I'd nailed it. Good; I was now going to be able to mend a few things, and even by hand, I could do a basic runner stitch because that's what the sewing machine stitching looked like on the fabric. Can't say I was any good at threading the needle, that really annoyed me.

Of course, I hadn't realised, I was only just about holding the two pieces of fabric together. If I had pulled on it, it would have come apart, but it still didn't matter to me. I was sewing and confident I would really master the art of it with practice. I had to; I simply couldn't keep walking about in ill-fitting worn-out shabby garments.

Learning to Trust and Bond with Others

They were great neighbours; they never once commented on our clothes and wanted to bond with us from day one apparently. No wonder Shazier was willing to stick up for me. I remember she insisted that they should wait or help me with Pam going to school; how nice was that?

Pure joy I felt after her suggestion. Great, somebody sticking up for me for once, and not me doing all the defending. It didn't materialise however, they still went on without us, but at least, I knew it was because they feared being late.

One turn of Sarah's head saying, "will you be alright?" Was more than enough reassurance that they now knew and realised I wasn't quite coping.

Everything changed; I still had to defend Pam every now and then at school, but there was no longer a need to ensure everyone knew not to mess with me.
Home life got less demanding; oh, the pressure cooker hat and the heavy yoke I wore was replaced with the equivalent of a matching cashmere hat and scarf. This, however, was a façade; the gentle, relaxed real me had to coincide???? inside once again. I would soon have to become even more stern than ever before, something deeper and seriously profound was to be highlighted. Mother had cancer.

I'm not sure when the mastectomy took place, only the aftermath of it. I recall quite clearly with horror when I came across her prosthesis breast, she, unfortunately, left it in the bathroom. I didn't know she had cancer, what was cancer anyway? Nobody ever said the word, they only said **'the big C.'** I don't know if she revealed it to any of us; knowing Mother, it was most likely kept quiet.

Father had type one diabetes, so we were already acquainted with district nurses. I did his feet on the quiet, and Jenna mainly did his insulin jabs until I got the knack practicing on the oranges, then it became our job together. We would pinch the orange with thumb and forefinger this was shown to Dad by the district nurses for himself to learn but he couldn't do it, it's a good thing we watched or how on earth would we have done it.

"I can't do it Daddy I'm too shaky,"

"yu havfe do it, Mi can't pinch me owna arm an push in de neegle!"

It's odd how we were both so frightened to hurt him, but he could beat us so hard without a thought and it was almost always Jenna and me. We were kids honestly, this really was too much.

In the afternoon, that I found Mother's prosthetic breast; Pam had chicken pox, so I was kept off school to help look after her at home as I'd already had it.
I went to the bathroom and there it was floating in a basin in the bath.

"The lumps now beginning to protrude from my chest will eventually fall off!" I thought and not at the same time because there was only one breast in the bowl. This was not going to happen to me, if they were going to fall off, maybe one day when I was running, in front of everybody, then they were not going to come at all, better off without them.

Everybody was different; from what I'd already seen, some had huge breasts bigger than their own heads. What if I had football bumps and one fell off, would I get the right size to float about in a bowl, dry out then stick back on? No way. It freaked me out, so I would tie them down from now on.

Using long pieces of crepe bandage, I began yet another ritual, binding those bumps down good and tight.

I studied my older sisters' chests with intensity, whose will fall off first? I watched the teachers and all the females in school, not sure how discreet I was, but it was all consuming, why on earth didn't Mom just speak to us?

Yes, everything certainly did change; sometimes I got very embarrassed because Mother would be lopsided, and I wasn't supposed to see that. I wasn't even supposed to be thinking about my Mother's breasts at all. A change occurred in the house; the atmosphere.

Mom and Dad began to go out; they would dress to the nines, silky gown rolled hair with fur coat, Dad, oh, he was so dapper, even had spats beautiful 1930s black and white slip over shoes with its own button-attached sock. I think they went out every week, obvious now that they were going to enjoy what time they had left.

Mom's treatment must have been successful; they must have got it all out because it was a few more years before we saw any deterioration and they continued to go out regularly.

Those years were the most exciting times of all. Mom went back to work calling bingo; she looks confident in the picture and she seemed to enjoy it too.

Our friendship with the neighbours and the bonus of school friendships meant we were all much calmer, more at peace with ourselves as well as each other. Some of the neighbours were not so friendly; however, that lot further up the road came into our little fold, fresh meat, lambs to the slaughter we were.

They began to try to manipulate us into stealing from the corner shops; we knew Dad had a good relationship with them because of the vegetables, so we were really scared. It was some years later before we could stand up to them and show our worth as it were, but they seemed to be okay by then.

Being friends with them, however, was never to be like the 'Begum' family and the 'Gayles,' the black and Asian families across the way. No, we were joined at the hips with them, happily too.

Being so creative, we organised a theatre production in the neighbourhood; it was an absolute joke, it was a mashup of The Wizard of Oz only with our own interpretation of added nursery rhymes or songs that we knew.

I can't remember the full extent of it, but it was quite the showpiece, to us anyway.

I got sewing, it was exciting, the costumes were brilliant, and as for our makeup, hey, we did ourselves proud.

We advertised it up and down the street, really thought we would be an overnight success, what a palaver!

A proper set of little entrepreneurs, we were, thinking we could charge a 2p entrance fee! In the end, we were begging the whole street to come, and we would feed them if they did, told you it was joke, but oh, what fun.

We split into two groups one for the street one for the grove, of course Muzzier was in my group we did everything with those neighbours. We were so nervous knocking on doors and ringing bells. Ding dong, our group hear someone coming guess who gets pushed to the front uhum. The door opens,

"hello sir, I'm Jannette Mr Joseph's daughter from 111, erm we're doing a little show in the grove about animals, would you please come we're making cakes!"

That was so scary to do but I got better at each door.

"That was good, do you think he might come?"

Sheila said, "I don't know do I, I don't know him."

Muzzier laughed her head off, we certainly had a lot of fun times with our newly adopted family; that's how they felt to us, just like family, only without the squabbles and tension. Weddings, birthdays, they are always the first contacted to join us and vice versa. My sister, Sarah, is good at all that keeping contact stuff; I'm not very good at that at all, I must admit.

Forty almost fifty come to think of it, years of friendships, the only genuine connection I have really had because they knew the depth of me.

We did such naughty things as children; besides the postman's knock, you know the one where you ring the bell or knock the letterbox then flee. Caused havoc stealing our neighbour's apples, rhubarb, gooseberries, there were pears too, but I didn't have them.

It was the trespassing that caused problems; we didn't give a hoot. If there were bear traps, we were still going in; nothing felt dangerous to us. We built 'dens' on their property, the kind only boys did back then, and roughed it all day.

Food was our stolen spoils, Shazier used to salt hers, I stole sugar from the jar at home and kept it in a glove, so I could use it anytime I pleased. We would pick fruit because it was there not because it was ripe, which more than often it wasn't giving us terrible stomach aches.

We were so oblivious to dangers; you know how derelict buildings were all over the place in the seventies. If you don't, they were, believe me; well they were our playgrounds too. Walking on loose floorboards, rickety stairs, not thinking we could have fallen through at any minute. We were rebels, feral kids, rampaging the neighbourhood and we couldn't care less.

Speaking of dangers, this one occasion is priceless. I'll set the scene for you. Imagine a large industrial estate with various factories all operating; the corner of the estate has a low wall, a set of unruly kids enter, looking for fun, that's us of course.

Now, some of these places have guard dogs, and it's a good thing this one didn't, or we would have been shredded. We come across what I now know would have been a clothing recycle van. I was going in, I wanted clothes more than anything in the world, but there were toys too, what a treasure trove.

As we dug deep, finding all sorts of wonderful clothes, toys, filling our arms with so much merchandise, we couldn't possibly carry let alone run with them. I came across something pink; the first thing was the ribbon. I pulled hard on the ribbon, half the stuff was so smelly too, but I didn't care and continued to pull.

"Ballet shoes," I shouted, "I found ballet shoes."

Keeping those ballet shoes over the years has been quite the talking point.

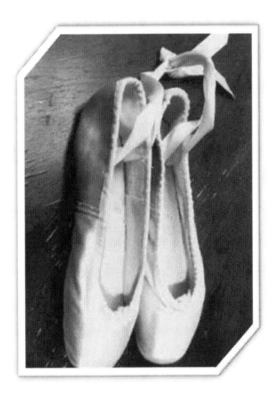

It may have been only Sheila and me that danced to start with, but by the time we were in our very late teens, early twenties, we were all at it.

"Oh no! There's only one, where's the other one?" I said, I looked and looked, dropping everything else.

"Somebody's coming" said Shazier and jumped out.

'Hide,' she said.

Did I hide? Not in hell did I, 'but I want that shoe,' I told her.

About a minute later, the door to the van slammed shut, my sister started to cry, she hid, but you know, I continued looking for the damn shoe. 'I got it,' and then realised the situation we were in, all those Sunday's in the church came in handy because, boy, we did pray.

It was a long time before we saw that door open, opened by Shazier. She must have kept close until the path was clear, phew! That was a real close shave. I laugh out loud every time I think of it, just goes to show what effect having all the leftover tatt had on me, talk about being caught red-handed.

My sewing skills developed, the urgency to have decent clothes was more than I could bear, so much, in fact, that I resorted to harnessing some fabric from 'waste matter.'

No, really, let me explain. We came across a pile of rubble on one of our escapades; this pile was full of glass, rubber, dog poop, waste paper, as well as the bits of broken furniture. Worst of all, it was prepared for burning. So, soaked with petrol, it was that the smell was toxic, but I spotted something. I spotted a multitude of different coloured polka dot material; blue, green, pink, and orange.

Oh my god, I was in my element. "I'm having the lot," I said, as I dug in, pulling and pulling different colours of it out.

"Come on," I said, 'help me, somebody wants to burn this, they mlight come back any minute.' The others joined in; oh, the smell was overwhelming, we didn't even think of the consequences of getting cut, the fabric was too beautiful.

When we pulled out as much as we could see, we wrapped it up under our jumpers and ran as fast as we could. At home, we saw we were alone; Dad was in the garden though, so we needed to do the washing of the fabric quick.

We filled the bathtub, got out the carbolic soap, and began to scrub and dip, scrub and dip, the air in the bathroom changed to smog, we opened the window and fanned it, it was like we were in a garage workshop, toxic fumes were everywhere, but the fabric was getting cleaner.

We filled the bath again and washed until we could no longer feel any slime, wow! We had ourselves a beautiful set of different coloured polka dot fabric that could be transformed into a new set of clothes.

We got away with it, we cleaned the bath out, the smell was still lingering, but the smell of paraffin was a constant odor anyway, and that was no joking matter, like sniffing led paint all day.

It wasn't long before I whipped up hot pants with waistcoats to match or the alternative swing skirt. For all my sisters and me, yes sir re!

We looked the business, in my original hand cut homemade fashion pieces. I did it; this was the most amazing feeling in the world. I knew I would never again look out of place, even if I continued to have hand me downs, it wouldn't matter.

I would now be confident enough to alter them to suit me, even if it meant turning the fabric inside out. I had to do that nearly all the time, but at least, instead of dreading what was handed to me, I relished the challenge and enjoyed picking at the seams to develop it.

The strange thing about that occasion is that Mom, even Dad, never batted an eyelid, never asked where these new clothes came from; so, me getting praised for it wouldn't come. My sisters, however, loved them, and I was queen bee for a short spell.

Mom and Dad knew I was talented and made me do even more stuff because I would get it right. Sarah enjoyed making cakes with Dad, Martha was always in the kitchen now, having to cook, the pendulum had swung in our direction, Dad was doing less apart from the gardening, his attention drawn to building two extensions to the house to accommodate Desmond.

Desmond had joined the Navy, by then, you see, and Dad wanted it built because he was very proud of him, plus he needed his own space. Desmond, Martha, and Sheila were now interested in the opposite sex, so Jenna, Sarah, Pam, and I all got closer; it was better, just us four.

Our relationships with the Begums and Sharon Gayle deepened; we played out for longer, had open window parties in the front room dancing about by the window to share our scene and music, by playing the gram loud indeed, oh yes happy days. Dad being on the other end of the house and our solidarity meant we were strong enough to face the whatever.

The extension was taking all of Dad's time. He needed help; you're not going to believe this, but we were his apprentices. We mixed cement using a proper adult shovel and carrying those heavy bags of sand and cement mix in a wheelbarrow, probably our own body weight, but it didn't stop there.

Poor Jenna was up and down the ladder with absolutely no safety equipment carrying bricks on her shoulders. My hands would crack from the cement mix; it really hurt, but we endured it to the very end. So proud he was of those extensions, our Dad.

When they were finished, we were able to put our stamp on it, a great big mural was painted on each of the extension walls, and soon Desmond moved in with his girlfriend. Martha was interested in one of the Begum brothers, and Sheila was just interested in boys, period.

It would only be a short while before she had a fella too, that's when Martha and Sheila got close, going out to discuss and such, really dressing up and wearing makeup.

At night, they would be sneaking in, funny, they were different people now, all grown up and we, we were just kids in their way, in their room; thank goodness we, at least, had bunk beds now.

They weren't the only ones who were different people now; Mom and Dad were changing too. The going out cut down, but it wasn't because Mom was getting ill again, in hindsight, it could have been. They were arguing again, and Mom's personality changed. It could have been the effects of the cancer returning and spreading; I don't know. I didn't stick around long enough, I only came back when Jenna got a place, to witness the decline in Mother and help care for her.

The fact that I only just begun to like myself, handle my life, we were still getting beatings, but a beating now reflected what was going on between them. It felt more like hatred, frustration, and not discipline. For the first time ever, I thought to myself; I could easily hold onto that strap, stick, or any other implement and whack Dad straight back.

One time, I was sleeping on the sofa upside down. I know, weird child. My sisters were sitting in the normal manner when 'whack' with the broom handle; Jenna had done something, but Dad missed her legs and got me on the head. One almighty coco bump raised like a volcano right on my temple, completely dazed me. Did he say sorry?

Of course, not, 'you shouldn't be in the way,' that was his reply.

It was then I knew I was not going to be able to tolerate that treatment much longer. I certainly didn't want to hit my father. I was now approaching eleven. By age fifteen, I'd gone, but only after a trial of leaving home for a week in which Mother called the police.

I was ready to strike Dad; I'd already jumped on the back of my brother for hitting Pam and throwing her against the front yard gate. Sheila confessed to me that Dad had done something quite severe to Desmond when he was about thirteen that maybe why he reacted that way to Pam I don't know, I do know that Dad made me want to hurt people if they annoyed me not that that's any excuse it was wrong of him period.

Nobody got away with hurting Pam, not by words or deeds. She was my ward, so to speak, from a baby and she couldn't help being different. He should have known better. I wanted to strangle him, but he threw me to the floor like his kit bag.

I had a lot of anger and resentment all settled, and both Desmond and Dad were reviving it, bringing it all back to the surface along with miss bossy boots. Only now I was bigger, stronger, and I understood things more. A dangerous combination not to be trifled with, remember my pressure cooker hat, well it was back in place, and it was steaming. I had something else to worry about; all too soon, another big change and yet another settling in for Pam. We were going to have to attend a big school.

I passed my eleven plus, but that didn't matter.

I would still have to go to the school my sisters attended and have their uniform.

I thought I would be attending Martha and Sheila's School, which was only for girls because, that's where I took the eleven plus test. But no, there wasn't a space for me there. I was going to Jenna and Sarah's school, which was mixed like an infant and junior school was.

I deserved to go to grammar school I worked so bloody hard and after all my setbacks to, but the cost of the uniform was too high, and you had to have a blazer plus a summer uniform and proper sports kit, it wasn't going to happen. I knew what was coming and took it on the chin. I didn't know then that going to that school would not only give me my first liaison with my now husband but allow me to know about a club called 'solar energy,' and from it, getting introduced to my first two children's father in the form of a dance-off.

Now, all that and more, you'll have to wait for in Part two of this trilogy along with me establishing myself in my new comprehensive secondary school, fighting my way to top dog in defense yet again of Pam, and excelling from the onset in the highest forms, they're all to come.

My leaving home, experiencing another form of abuse as well as childbirth and homelessness. Why I chose to write my autobiography will become more and more clear to you. My name is **Jannette Barrett**; thank you for walking with me. I hope we meet again in books two and three.

Afterword

By
Jannette Barrett

I don't think I have the right to use the phrase by God, but I wish you to understand the enormity of what I have endured writing my memoirs. 'IT IS FINISHED'

If, but I hope it's when you purchase my second book containing parts two and three due to reading this, even if simply out of sheer curiosity, I'm hoping that you find when a person takes the step to write about their life many many questions are first thought through. I hope you appreciate the craft that goes into it as well as the effects that the elements of regression can cause.

There is so much that can be targeted or achieved using the correct words written appropriately. It can be to the receiver the likeness of wearing a soft cashmere sweater on a cold day.

Have the sharpness of a sword to cut through targets of oppression or be the vows a couple promise to each other on their wedding day.

My words may have spelt, pain, anguish, disillusionment disgrace, guilt, self-loathing, selfishness and disregard, but it also spelt out.
Love, contentment, astonishment, excitement, belief, faithfulness, awareness, motivation, success, hope, relief and promise.

Writing became my morphine drive that cut out the pain to the cancerous past that plagued me, it released a strength within me I didn't know I had. Yes, it was difficult, yes it hurt like hell and at times I wanted to cease writing, but I so wanted my freedom more.

As my third and final part depicts. TRUTH IS MY FREEDOM. It has been, and I am finally in flight.

I am hoping you found my style of writing easy to read, and the counsel helpful. It's been quite an encounter for me, and I'm pleased I've started my own healing with the help of The Almighty. If you stopped and found it less than stimulating, then thank you still for purchasing it.

I was a nurse, but I am now a community carer. I've done live in care for years on end, worked in hospitals as well as nursing and residential homes.

I am best suited, however, to the one-to-one care within an individual's own home, and now, I wonder why that is! I stated from the start that my sister, was the making of me; what do you now think after you've read this first part of my life?

See you in my future then, maybe, where you will read how the development of patience from childhood has served me well throughout my life.
I have included a picture of me on a symbolic throne, to depict my triumph over the demons I have fought when finding myself during this regression to childhood.

Many years of unanswered questions, digging deep to surrender the past, live in the now and move forward.

Why I Chose to Write Rather Than Block

I am sure you have heard of the phrase, "One step forward two steps back."

It's an 'IDIOM' meaning a continuation of backward stepping from achievement to un-achievement. Life can be like that sometimes, a series of opportunities resulting in failures. Failure, although a setback, is also a lesson and a valuable one at that. As we get older, we tend to make more and more rash decisions perhaps.

Why do I think this?

I think so because I believe we fear that we're running out of time so grab chances with both hands no matter how futile, and the thinking that we can make it work!

When it fails to materialise, we often slump, I for one fear failure more the older I get, but I'm not afraid to admit that.

Apparently, when you're young and vibrant, you feel invincible because you're not usually given any form of responsibility; therefore, you enjoy that youthful ride of your life quite rightly so.

But you would normally expect someone to grow out of that mindset and not continue chasing rainbows achieving nothing in their lifetime.

Choosing not to do anything allowing life to just pass us by, would be a complete waste. Not much point in saying at death's door, 'why didn't I do that sooner.'

So yes, many of us will continue to try no matter how many times we fall then look back at our childhood with a longing for those carefree days when it wouldn't have mattered if we did fall because we had time on our side.

For me, the pen and ink have always hit the paper, but the choice to write about my life materialised only after I realised that I needed my healing and a reference point to analyse my life experiences.

You may be wondering what I mean by, 'why I chose to write rather than block.'

Well, as far as I can recall and believe me that's pretty far back, I was taught to hide my feelings due to my circumstances, this continued incubating of my emotions completely suppressed me, so much so I could no longer identify who the hell I was later on in my life.

I can't say I handled the circumstances I faced very well because of all the harbouring, one little lip tremble or chin wobble made me think I was weak, so I punished myself on a regular basis, and I did it in the harshest of ways.

As a young woman, due to many years of complex issues faced, I had to undergo counselling therapy. Now unbeknown to me some of the methods taught me I had already used.

The counsellor taught me three valuable primary lessons amongst others, of which I've retained. Without those fundamental lessons I'm sure I would have struggled through life even more than I have.

Lesson One - To accept who I was.

Now I was nearly always pretending, acting my way into acceptance. When I heard that sentence spoken, I felt my heart leap; someone was willing me to be me, could they see who I was?

Lesson Two - To believe I could learn and grow from any given situation.

Learn and grow! What did she mean? I knew I was interested in learning anything I could to make my life better; for my dreams to become realities. As for growth could that mean I would move on! My life of shit was just temporary!

That got me excited, and I listened intently at the various methods to get me on the right track to that growth.

Lesson Three - To acknowledge the season I was in. Lesson Three was as clear as mud to me. Seasons were, Spring, Summer, Autumn and Winter, of course, I knew what season I was in, now I just got cross believing she thought I was thick until she started to try and explain it as a period in my life.

Explaining that at the age I was I shouldn't have been experiencing any of it, agreeing that it was most unfortunate that I should be trying to handle it alone.

Did all the points within those lessons make much sense to me at the time? Yes and no. Lessons, 1 and three were harder to come to terms with but like I said, lesson 2 interested me, so I began to acknowledge my behaviour and deal with the reckless, destructive ways I punished myself by not coping, I did this almost immediately.

Over the next thirty plus years, all three lessons began to make sense as I battled various issues. When you've been trained to be on the back burner most of your life, it's not easy to open up and shed light on what's truly you.

Within the counselling, I was also taught to list my negatives and positives, and next to each one of them try to explain why I felt it was either.

My explanations of why I felt a particular way was depicted as a series of drawings mainly in thick black crayon, doodling circles of frustrated anger was my most common, and with it I drew all the ugly faces I could pull at myself in the mirror, there wasn't that much writing at all if I'm honest.

Next to my positives were usually clouds in the sky or trees and flowers, I so wanted to be free, those type of drawings gave me that feeling of freedom although brief.

I always knew then why I felt the way I did but had no methods of how to handle my feelings indeed not the right words, but I did try to write them down.

The counsellor was getting me to do something similar, but this time there would be no black crayons to hide behind she had to help me find the best methods suitable for me and of course be age-related.

I didn't write much before, but it did always help me, now I would be taught how to write down my feelings correctly which wasn't going to be easy for me or draw it more specifically.

I had to as I found it difficult to say out loud how I felt, sometimes I was completely lost of voice due to being unable to have my say or voice my opinions for so long.

Who I was the true authentic me was always being crushed, swallowed up, but you wouldn't have thought so if you saw how I would act, so to have the opportunity to speak up, say how I felt, ask for what I needed, what! This was genuinely foreign territory for me.

The counsellor was good, good at her job. She had a way of prising out my truths by allowing me to ask myself what I would say or do, she made me feel in charge and get to grips with my issues.

I may be of the minority when I say I understand why people feel the need to air their laundry in a downwind; it's often either a cry for help or a complete relief to get rid of what ails them that they no longer care of the consequences.

I can't say I'm a 'Jerry Springer' or 'Jeremy Kyle' type guest as I'm not a 'shout it from the rooftops' person.

Speaking about my problems isn't my thing at all, I'm very private indeed, so to release myself from decades of parasitic memories, I chose to write them out rather than blocking them in any longer, and that sounds completely contradictory to the private person I just said I am.

It brings home just how vital and highly necessary the need was for me to come to terms with my past once and for all by finding my healing references.

Now you know the reason I chose to write about my life, the good and the bad rather than block in parts like it never existed, denying who I was and what I have experienced.

Here is how I unravelled my jigsaw, linked all the pieces to find the book within me.

Back then I was so confused, to descramble my confusion with the use of my imagination I'd write, well I say write, but it was more a combination of those cloud image drawings, with a few words of what they meant to me and lists. Was that the start of my rhythmical writing?

I'm not sure but I know I was always doing things for myself quickly, merely because there wasn't ever much time to do my things so doing part writing and part drawings where I could see the story I wanted and remember it was ideal.

I was also an accurate mimic having a real thirst to learn and improve myself, so I would try to develop each story as I discovered new things.

Negatives Against Positives.

In my youngest years, I was resentful, angry, I felt forgotten about, invisible and that made me anxious at times, but because of the position I was placed in I was also well proud, happy, which made me feel resourceful and important.

It was the battle of those negatives against positives, that started an epidemic virus within me that's taken decades to control, its antidote was my writing and counselling.

We can all sense bad vibes can't we! That's why the memory tends to draw on the negative experiences we have and thrive. Well, my initial first experience and realisation of being overlooked as a child was the onset of my personality change, I'm sure of it. I describe it to the likeness of Japanese knotweed in part one because its deep roots were like the harmful spores that spread quickly through me.

'LESSON 1' from my counsellor, accepting who I am helped me face those painful memories, embrace that imaginary part of me that could just say anything just as it was and write it down. That acceptance also prevented me returning to the pain of the pram, that waiting and never getting, I had to want to fix me I couldn't wait any longer for someone to do it for me.

I realise that my circumstances made me change and fight against who I was to try and become someone else, being overlooked was not nice; I wished I knew how to embrace my emotions and go with the flow of them, whether angry, glad, happy or sad so I developed more evenly. Warning to self, never try to be who you are not.

Oh those positive memories of Euphoria, pleasure, joy they were few and far between but when they came I quickly absorbed them and shared them with my sisters, that's how I was, with them always wanting their approval so if ever I found something that I considered exciting or interesting I'd try to involve them so we could do it together and I would feel 'normal'.

Those positive times filled me up like a satisfactory dinner, warmed me up nicely but then they would fade away just like watching a sunset, leaving me with an essence of endorphins and a very pleasant sigh.

I don't know why our most united times as a family never seemed to last very long because when we did something together, it was brilliant.

At the back of my mind I knew my worth even then but only with the strength of my sisters, alone I felt like nothing we were all very creative, I'm smiling now as I write this because the impact of that time was epic. Have you noticed yourself start to smile, even laugh when you recall positive, pleasant memories even before you begin to tell someone the tale?

Isn't it a nice feeling! It's a pity however that 'nice' can quickly be replaced with stale complacency when too many negatives outweigh them.

Negative suppression doesn't sleep that's why it's always hovering with intent; those deep-roots and spores I stated earlier spread a virus within that plagues the incubator.

If that happens to be you, it indeed was me, and it's not dealt with, literally cut out, it eats at your core until it morphs you into something equally ugly, you can then end up neither recognising or relating to yourself and become lost.

It's so important to have choices, and everyone should have an element of it even if not quite compos-mentis it's our human right after all. I've chosen to write pure and simple.

Believe it or not, it's probably one of the easier choices I've ever made because my early years were based on sheer guesswork and speculation resulting in my interpretations to life being way off balance. I had no idea how to weigh up the 'pros or cons.' With these confused interpretations ingrained, I developed even more layers of that negative suppression because of being left to my own devices.

I changed personality to survive, that was my affirmation that I had wholly and finally reached the pinnacle of self-control and equilibrium.
The pen and ink speaking my life on the page made me complete, and I was able to continue chapter after chapter.

If I hadn't ventured valiantly into the depth of myself to draw out my parasitic past, deal with it, analyse it and write it down to free myself, I would still have only a vague understanding of who the hell Jannette Barrett is.

I visualised my past as an incubated maggot working its way through me, seeing it that way helped because a maggot must eventually become a fly and take off, I certainly wanted to free my past and therefore me. It has been a battle to recall all I encountered and what I ended up doing to survive to then accepting the person I am, but it's so worth it now.

All that the anger and frustrations did was deceive me, and it lowered my self-esteem further making my self-confidence practically non-existent.

I couldn't continue like that and didn't want to be hating myself the way I did with a passion because I couldn't deal with all the confusion in my life, but I kept sliding resulting in me becoming a 'Jekyll and Hyde,' being that way distorted me; diluting my essence leaving me with no balance whatsoever. I was so erratic I didn't know how to switch off.

I still to this day carry that type of overload factor; now I call it 'my do it yourself gene' disguising it as something miraculous when I know oh too well just how destructive it can be.

Of course, it stems from not having much help so early on in life and being left to my own devices, so it's rather sad when people say to me "wow! I don't know how you manage to keep going" a smile is usually all I can manage as a reply, it wasn't an easy task writing about how low I got at those times; the things I did and said when in those states of disparity.

Colleagues today still tell me to slow down and try to think of myself and I'm much better at delegation but caring roughly from the tender age of three, unfortunately I've got that forced blueprint well and truly embedded; it's like the knot in the wood of the tree, no matter how far you push or file me down the knot/blueprint is a constant birthmark throughout, it's not easy to erase . Very difficult to bend a fully-grown tree.

Those early years, I'm telling you nobody could get close, not for the want of trying though. I was carrying a dark secret that I didn't understand or comprehend. It made me more adamant I wasn't going to allow anyone to impregnate me with any form of doctrine, good or bad not that I could even have judged it correctly. Being so utterly fed up with not having any choice, I fixed my mindset to not be influenced.

All those years of being left to my own devices made me stubborn, and I certainly pushed people away before they tried to push me, I was always in some form of fighting.

It didn't even matter if I made a mistake either, you know why!

They never bloody checked that's why, if they did perhaps certain things wouldn't have happened. I always seemed to look as though I was coping part of my constant concealing; I couldn't even stop myself from doing it; certainly, didn't mean I was coping or wanted to.

I felt I should have been treated with rewards for what I had to both give up in my life and for all I had to put up with, but no rewards ever came, so I became very resentful. That pill is bitter when swallowed.

Writing how I felt has been hard because the truth of the matter is, the way my life planned out especially the duties given to me was actually the making of me, but it was only as an adult I could recollect that, and the guilt almost sent me over the precipice because I could be ruthless over things.

There's been a great deal of regurgitation in the last few paragraphs hasn't there?

So you are probably wondering by now how I managed to cope while writing, I've said it wasn't easy, but I haven't told how I coped.

The black crayon circles, for instance, that was mainly because I wasn't that good at putting my thoughts down in writing early on in life, the reason for that is because I live with dyslexia, you will come to read the reasons why my education was

floored and the only way to catch up was for me to take my work home and try using my own methods to complete it.

You should see how my children laugh at the way I go around the mulberry bush to calculate the basic arithmetic but I'm okay with that because I'm proud of the way I coped, in my day there was enough to do at home already with all my share of chores etcetera.

To think at one time I felt I had no voice, now you'll find it hard to shut me up or to stop me expressing my opinions, it's a far cry from my earliest pictorial or metaphorical expression to compensate for my lack of English language writing, I write in droves now, in fact, I would almost overly explain when I write just, so I was sure it was understood. I suppose you've noticed that already, it's certainly seen on my social media page.

Having an image to think about also allows me to remember what I was supposed to be writing about. You will see this type of style throughout the book even some makeshift counselling tips.

It's been my way of counselling myself through the parts of the book that I found difficult to write; all of it my own unique way of coping.

I sat on it, my complete disarray of mumbo jumbos, placed 'my life' in a shoe box and pushed it under the bed and I felt okay about all the things I had emptied. I read the jumbled jigsaw puzzle many times but being the private person, I am plus the utmost respect I have for my siblings, and the extended family, something very profound would have to happen before anyone else was going to see any of it.

I was writing for me myself and I, that's it, I needed it, it was my Morphine drive my drug of survival, and I had my doses dripped into my veins until I felt a level of acceptance of all I was and am.

As a firm believer of everything falling in its time and many years before I even started the process of attempting writing my memoirs, I was quite ill, but I pulled through.

Now that to some people should have been the right time to do the story of their life, but I couldn't.

Part of the pain I endured for many years was because of family, and they were still very much alive and kicking not only that, I now had children who looked up to me, a job with vulnerable clientele, how could I appear to be someone unstable?

No, I passed through my childhood triumphant, my teenage years although I prayed for the ground to open up and swallow me ample times, I sustained them, and there was no way as an adult I was going to upset the apple cart now.

Family acceptance was something I craved, to allow all I knew, all I had felt, all that had happened come to light while the main culprit still lived was something I couldn't and wouldn't do but then the year 2015 arrived. That year a specific family member died, and I found myself standing on the pulpit declaring that "The wages of sin is death" - Romans chapter 6 verse 23 in the Bible. All the family was present the elders the youngest ones the cousins and second cousins, but I walked to that pulpit, and I said what I said and knew what I meant when I said it.

After I'd finished expressing the message within the message within the message of that scripture, I went on to sing from the pit of my stomach, 'It is well with my Soul'.

I finally felt strong enough to stand alone and declare that I was now ready to speak. From that death came my life in print.

The year 2015 was my turning point, it was my time, and it was the right time, the outer family members who would be affected by all the reveal had become less relevant in the comparison.

I know now it couldn't have been at any other point in my life, so I started to piece my jigsaw together and create my Autobiographical Trilogy 'Sixth out of Seven'.

Going through all the diaries, bits of paper etcetera and reading them, what came to light was that the chameleon I'd become by camouflaging myself to create common ground with folk; pitifully desperate to be noticed and fit in, was a necessary act.

I was quite the fraud, that fraudulent character was what folk seemed to like and wanted more of. I found it easy to create an imaginary concoction of various influences that I mimicked because it was accepted. If only I was brave enough to show the real side of me, the one now writing.

I so wanted the ordinary inquisitive me to be seen. Back then I was completely invisible, shrouded in the cloak of pretence.

There was one thing I was sure of, however, even in my weakness, that I wasn't prepared to keep getting the leftovers, keep having to wait my turn, just put up and shut up, no!

I had more than enough of that, so I gave in to the pretence and allowed myself to morph fully into the ruling character personalities as I felt I would be swallowed up in the background if I didn't.

Here came the bossy boots alter egos, cocky, arrogant, self-opinionated survivors; my allies as well as my saboteurs all in one. Are they still present within me! Damn, right they are, well how could I be authentically me without the strong as well as the weak.

Great thing now is that although one character is the feisty dragon within, it presents itself as an asset and a huge comfort to me just like it was in my very tender years before the traumas of care and various issues took hold and started to weave into my life.

To know that I was that character all along and would have grown quite the confident assertive go get it, person, much earlier if not faced with the many things I'd endured, felt like I'd emerged the Phoenix from the furnace with a vibrant display of peacock plumage quite an exhilarating revelation of acknowledgement, writing did that.

Each stage through our lives we face scenarios of risk and being intuitive helps us weigh up the odds, for or against.

As there are risks in everything, we are going to come up short at times some more than others; without taking any, we wouldn't get very far in life though, would we?

After all, none of us want to live with regrets saying things such as, 'I'll never know because I failed to try.' It is yet to be acknowledged whether my choice to write proves to be too high a risk. Right now, I don't regret it at all as the benefits have honestly been great.

I know firsthand that I've experienced a great deal and overcame my initial Goliath, many besides me have also endured and overcome theirs. Is that it! Have I, therefore, equipped myself to overcome all that crosses my path with poison darts, of course not, realistically it's the continuous stepping over that I must endure to gain stability and conquer my past hurting.

With my own book to refer to as a reminder of how I stepped on those hot coals, broken glass, crossed over on tightropes with nothing to balance with but sheer grit and the will not to be crushed; dug myself trenches but also found ways out of them to my truths, my own pathway to healing and enlightenment shows, I must continue to be my own working progress and not let up on improving myself we are after all, flawed.

There were indeed times I could have given my arrogant self a damned good slap. Have you ever caught yourself saying or doing something and thought 'what the! Why did I say or do that?

The fact I knew I had so much to reign in and contend with made me even more determined to have something to refer to. The need to write my story became more and more apparent for my self-analysis. I saw it as my therapeutic resource the more it began to piece together.

Writing poetry for other people was always welcomed and appreciated, they found it healing I did to, so if I braved to find my truths amongst the memories and discover after many years who the hell I was, how much more along the pathway could I go in finding my light, my freedom, and my resolution.

As I read the accounts of my life then recalled many more and began to craft them into the book, it was very daunting especially when I had to try and write things about my parents and siblings having no idea what demon memories they may have been harbouring I mean, I blocked them for so long how could I be sure I wasn't misjudging what I was remembering with my emotions running so high!.

I had to tread carefully so as not to push myself over the edge recalling and also trying to be respectful of my family history. Writing also made me acknowledge what I was really good at in my life there is an enrichment when one makes the discovery of their purpose and continues to thrive on it, as it gives them the reason to continue.

Life without a purpose feels empty and lifeless, to function that way leads to inevitable isolation and lack of fulfillment.

An individual is not just skin deep; life isn't usually a bed of roses for the masses. Oh, those that appear to skip along on the fragrant petals and we, the so-called ordinary folk look upon their lives and can only dream of the grandeur, they can often end up with many a regret or need rehab just like any other individual.

That outer exterior doesn't reveal the depth of character so when we read about certain people, we aspired to perhaps be like and then we symbolically prick ourselves on those very thorns that carried the rose petals they skipped on because we tried to emulate them, we shouldn't be surprised that we bled like an artery in shock when they fell.

We have more of a realistic view of life than many of those people because we live at grassroots. It isn't rosy, because we don't go around in red tinted glasses obscuring our visions.

Well, I haven't got an entourage to guide and protect or encapsulate me, have you? You and I must face life head-on, go it alone as it were, and we should all have a sense of pride when we are able to do so, even if we make mistakes.

When I began this back in 2015, I said to myself, 'Where on earth do I start?' I didn't write straight away I couldn't. I began, however, to just try and dream, even meditate.

The therapeutic influence it brought me the way it helped me see how far I had come, how much I had already written although scrambled, outweighed the fear of the pen.

I didn't know how to format my writing into a book I knew what I understood, but what made sense to me wouldn't be eligible to anyone else especially my pictures and possibly my metaphorical expression, but the urge was intense so I 'struck at the iron while hot'.

The more I delved into my subconscious hidden child, the more in-depth things appeared and the prouder I became of myself especially on those revelations I stated earlier.

'Did I really get through that!' With more revelations and affirmations of my strengths seen right in front of me on those little pieces of scrap paper, my history was powerful, so I started to write the connective pieces to join what I had already hidden in the shoebox under the bed and brought out into the light.

Sometimes they would be quite sudden out of the blue memories of a missing link to the jigsaw I'd purposefully forgotten, and I'll have to write it down on anything at hand in fear that the vivid image and accuracy would fade again and be left as the watered-down version from the shoebox.

On a good day sentences came first then full paragraphs, each one prompted another, unscrambling a dusty, forgotten library of hidden truths now jumping right at me with so many unanswered questions. This cemented the fact that everything has its time because the minute I was sure I should write everything on my way home from the funeral, it started to flow, and I saw my way, I had indeed made the right decision to 'write rather than block'.

It no longer mattered to me that I feared the potential backlash, of course, my family and others would ask 'Why make my personal life public after all these years and bring shame,' as for my immediate family they went through the same traumas as me, they too received no instructions and I wasn't the only one that experienced some sensitive inexplicable things, although it was just me as the carer for at least fifteen years.

I spoke to them during this journey, and I have their blessing.

This was entirely for me when I started, then as I got deeper into writing it, the media was reporting on issues within my book and women were coming forward about certain encounters in their lives and it was like a massive ray of light to me, a significant affirmation that my story may even help someone else or many.

The dissecting to get raw, get real, elaborate on the many pieces of my written history and finally face every part of it head-on, then transfer it to a readable book took all of my self-control and it was as a drug, easing out the correct amount of writing and analysis on each part of my history as I answered my 'what ifs, maybes and should haves' each day as a form of pain relief. That's why I called my writing 'my morphine drive.'

To walk through the memories in true technicolour, when quite frankly it would have been more comfortable being left in the black and white version I first saw and wrote down or made a picture of because that was certainly easier to muster; but it was truth I sought after, so the walk, even though at times it felt like being barefoot on broken glass was justifiable.

Some memories were so cruel to recall they slapped me in the face like a frozen wind and I couldn't catch my breath; those ones were as nightmares.

I'd struggle to come away from them feeling paralysed in trance with my mind traveling quickly skipping years back and forth, such a kaleidoscope of disarray to compose myself from.

My eyes would still be fixed open at times with salted tear track marks on my cheeks from crying as I re-engaged with the present.

Starting the book made my mind wide open when your memories randomly reveal their unwanted secrets at the most inconvenient of times, it's like singing an annoying song off the radio, you even seem to know the words, and it surprises you.

How dare it creep in like dry rot and not stop no matter what you do to distract yourself from it, so unbelievably irritating.

Why do our most damaging memories do that? I think it's because we haven't dealt with them properly or found closure to them.

Unfortunately, some will never receive that curtain closure; I've depicted my most damaging as a vinyl record purposefully scratched so that it jumps and stops revealing everything.

Hopefully, over a period of time I will find that I no longer recollect its memory accurately not enough to do me any real damage; at least because some of the words and pictures will be missing from that scratch out, I gave it. It sounds an odd act to do but it's my way, and it helps.

I really wanted to write my whole truth and nothing but my whole truth, I am, however, no matter what you are now reading quite the coward to reveal to all and sundry.

What about feedback! People can be harsh critics, well my need to write was greater than that expectation so if yours isn't I urge you to, first, weigh up your own need against your fears and do what your gut spills out. It has been of a therapeutic benefit to me, so I do hope if you chose to write rather than block as I have, it does you justice to.

Nobody I know ever likes a maybe, we can all deal better with a definite yes or no. My life was full of these maybes, the need to have them answered was also a priority so whatever comes now from my book it's okay because those that are in my personal life have seen it, have seen my change, have appreciated my change, more importantly I have finally accepted the true authentic me because of it.

It was scary of course to be looking in the mirror at myself, the regurgitated mess I was vomiting up facing my demons, I must admit it to you and apologise that in the need to find a way to palletise it all, I resorted to a slight amount of fiction, mainly name changes and sometimes.

I didn't want to go any further than that because I felt I wouldn't be respecting myself or my true family history, after all, I did choose to write rather than block anything didn't I.

My Autobiographical Trilogy is full of twists and turns, and I was even told by someone that I was a 'marvel and had more to give than I thought', 'pearls of wisdom' if you like. I certainly don't claim to have any such thing, some glass beads maybe which aren't worth much but I'm willing to share them with you.

That's why within my writing I've tried to give some of the counselling tips I was given along with my metaphors, so you have a picture to draw on. I know there are 'triggers' within my book so I am mindful of not delving into too much graphical detail.

If you the reader purchases my second book containing parts two and three of my autobiography and resonate with any of the issues I faced, you will have your own memories, that I'm sure is enough to recall.

Mine is only meant to count as a reference that I hope with all my heart can help you and anyone else come to terms and find their pathway to freedom. The incubated true self, the one hidden because it feels it's not accepted, feels it is suppressed so often doesn't get the chance to fully shine, I've related this as a person's pilot light.

Writing helped me oxygenate my pilot light and re-combust to feel the fullness of my fire again. If I stayed the way, I was, harbouring, denying, this could have been a recipe for one or several forms of mental health issues. Maybe I should be considered at 'risk;' I know I'm doing my best not to become yet another statistic. It's a finer line than we may realise.

Today, there is more awareness, but it's still very hush-hush in certain cultures. My poetry I've said before has helped people, so I live in hope that my book will do the same.

Me embracing my entire self within this writing process thinking that it was only my voice of reason character that could ever be brave enough to air thoughts, the snippets that slept in the shoebox under the bed and then my dramatic walk to the pulpit have finally culminated into fruition.

Jannette

More About The Author

A few words about me, totally biased of course as it's written by my husband Paul.

"Jannette Barrett, nee Joseph, aka Ms Lyricist 'B,' has truly overcome. I am amazed she has the ability to remember detailed accounts of her childhood, especially as this part of her trilogy, 'Triumphant through my early years' is based only on ages 3-11 years.

I am her second husband, and I have full account of her strength and endurance through some seriously tough times. She depicts me as her rock, her king. I am humbled by that statement. As she is indeed my Queen, my backbone. My huge regret in life is that I had not the maturity, or the confidence to take her on when the chance was before me. I was her very first love interest.

I missed the opportunity to have been, the biological father of all our children, especially as I believe the one, she lost wouldn't have passed if I was the father. She is a wonderful selfless woman, who keeps on giving, I feel so incredibly blessed that she chose me.

My wife runs her own care in the community company called 'JAN CAN CARE' with the aid of family members tirelessly. She has strong faith and exceptional resilience. Thank you for your support of her, with the purchase. **Paul Barrett**

This is a picture of my husband Paul with our son Dominic taken in 1993 uniting our family unit.

Editorial & Reader Reviews for

Triumphant Through My Early Years by Jannette Barrett.

...This is a Very Compelling Read...

I am delighted to review part one of Jannette's autobiography. Her book charts her formative early years, growing up as a first generation British daughter to Jamaican parents, in a large Jamaican family. Jannette is the 6th child out of 7 children yet she was the sole carer to her younger sister Pam, who had her challenges. Her journey is told eloquently by her 4 year old self.

The reader is taken through Jannette's harsh upbringing in Handsworth in Birmingham, marked by physical abuse, where she is overlooked and where her emotional and physical needs are not met. Although she enjoys a short reprieve when she starts school, it is clear that this is enough to start Jannette's thirst for learning, education and sparks her creativity.

Jannette's recollection of physical and historical child sexual abuse are so painful you can feel it, I could have easily cried. Conversely, there are endearing moments as she recalls watching her father make dumplings for Saturday soup are heart warming. This is a very compelling read so far and I wish Jannette every success with her book.

Pamela R Haynes - Multi- Award Winning & Best-Selling Author

Soul Strong!

A harrowing read told with dignity and truth. I could feel the author walking with me whilst reading this raw account of childhood.

Although I thoroughly enjoyed reading and getting to know why the author wrote this first book of the series, I couldn't wait to get to the story itself. I worry that some readers may skip through and therefore it would be missed.

The content and style of the manuscript is very strong, I was triggered into a thought-provoking process that may have a profound effect on some readers. Janette as sparked an interest in me wanting to read the next book and the one after, I got hooked, wanting to read more and more.

As seen above I have titled my readers review as Soul Strong. This read is told from deep within the soul and I felt it grow with strength and confidence even within this early years first account. The soul strong also know when it is time to let go of something that no longer serves them, I believe this read to support the souls looking for strength in finding self through dark and trying life events.

Overall this manuscript left me with relatable, real, deep emotions that impact to the very core of our foundations.

Shelly Allmark – Editorial Reviewer

I Love this Story.

It captured my imagination as I lived in the moment too. As it felt like I was right there too. Wishing I could reach out and rescue a soul so pure and precious.

It wowed me to know that Jannette remembered detailed parts of her life from the age of three. A must read as the Author goes back and remembers her childhood from the age of three, remembering the abuse and responsibilities for her younger sister. T

he story captured me as the Author tells the story that has never before told. Well done Jannette you brave and courageous beautiful being. You've built an inner strength no one can tear down now. Can't wait to read the rest of the story in the books to come. Thank you for sharing.

Yanique Taylor-Francis - Author and Beauty Specialist

A Word from The Publisher

Dear Jannette,

What courage, what honesty and such detail, the development of the book was an epic journey in and of it self.

We were challenged, stretched out of our comfort zones, we cried and laughed along the way.

I've lived with your story in my heart since the first night I read your draft.

I know this book will shock and disturb but ultimately it will help others as it has helped you and I.

Thank you for trusting me with your life story.

Marcia M.

Marcia M Spence
CEO Marcia M Publishing House

Triumphant Through My Early Years by Jannette Barrett.

Marcia M Publishing House is a Socially Responsible Publisher.

If you or someone you know has been affected by any of the issues contained in this book, please contact your local child protection services and or vulnerable adult services. You can find a list of National Helplines on our Website.

Marciampublishing.com

12062714R00125

Printed in Great Britain
by Amazon